D0598706

SUNDAY CASSEROLES

SUNDAY CASSEROLES

Complete Comfort in One Dish

BETTY ROSBOTTOM | *photographs by* SUSIE CUSHNER

CHRONICLE BOOKS

SAN FRANCISCO

Text copyright © 2014 by Betty Rosbottom.
Photographs copyright © 2014 by Susie Cushner.
All rights reserved. No part of this book may be reproduced in any
form without written permission from the publisher.

Library of Congress Cataloging-in-Publication Data available.
ISBN 978-1-4521-2120-8

Manufactured in the USA

Prop styling by Heather Crowther
Food styling by Dana Bonagura
Typesetting by Bruce A. Purdy

Campari tomatoes is a registered trademark of Mastronardi Produce Ltd.
McCormick is a registered trademark of McCormick and Co.
Pyrex is a registered trademark of Corning Inc.
Tabasco is a registered trademark of McIlhenny Co.
Wondra flour is a registered trademark of General Mills, Inc.

10 9 8 7 6 5 4 3

Chronicle Books LLC
680 Second Street
San Francisco, California 94107
www.chroniclebooks.com

For my husband, who brings love, encouragement,
and a sense of humor to our table.

ACKNOWLEDGMENTS

Many people shared their time and talents with me as I worked on this project, and their suggestions, comments, and enthusiasm have enriched this book.

My editor, Bill LeBlond, came up with the idea for another "Sunday" book, proposing casseroles as the theme. There aren't enough words of gratitude for his wise advice and support.

I am lucky to have as my agent Lisa Ekus, who believes in my work and whose incredibly dedicated staff always finds new ways to promote it.

Thanks to my longtime assistants, Emily Bell and Mary Francis, for being essential to the completion of yet another culinary marathon. Emily helped invent new casseroles and update traditional ones, while Mary took charge of all the volunteer testers, and also used her outstanding computer skills to instantly refine the recipes and text.

Ron Parent and Diana Tindall tested casseroles in my kitchen for the better part of a year, and Betsey Wolfson joined in for the hectic last few months. Sheri Lisak and Barbara Morse both fine-tuned recipes once they were in draft form.

Volunteers around the country cooked casseroles, month after month, and then wrote helpful reviews. They are truly the culinary angels team. Special thanks go to Wendy Ninke and Betty Orsega, and also to Marilyn Cozad, Marilyn Dougherty, Penny Schacht, Jackie Murill, Kent Faerber, Julia Hanley, Janet Hontanosas, Cindy Kurban, and Carroll Vuncannon.

Carrie Harmon, a new friend and wordsmith extraordinaire, took time from her busy life to help me find my voice and to make my words shine.

I offer deep gratitude to the editorial staff at Chronicle Books, who take my electronic manuscripts and turn them magically into beautiful books. I am privileged to work with such a talented team. Thanks especially go to Amy Treadwell for her skill and guidance, and to Deborah Kops for her careful copyediting. Thanks to Sarah Billingsley, Peter Perez, David Hawk, Doug Ogan, Sara Schneider, and Steve Kim. Thanks also to talented photographer Susie Cushner, food stylist Dana Bonagura, and prop stylist Heather Crowther for such beautiful photographs.

I am blessed with a wonderful family, who never complained this year when I brought casseroles to our Thanksgiving, Christmas, and Easter celebrations. Most of all, though, I sing praises to my husband, who sampled countless casseroles—both disasters and triumphs—always with an encouraging word, and who was never too tired to edit, with his professorial eye, another page of text.

CONTENTS

Introduction

"A good marriage is like a casserole; only those responsible for it really know what goes into it!"

—ANONYMOUS

Casseroles, like Proust's famous madeleines, evoke fond memories. Mention the word *casserole*, and most will describe, often in detail, their favorite all-in-one dish. Some swoon at the thought of their mother's creamy mac and cheese or glorious lasagna. Others become wistful as they talk of tuna noodle casseroles covered with a layer of crushed potato chips taken hot from the oven. My husband smiles when he remembers his father's baked enchiladas filled with chiles and cheese. And those of us who have been cooking for several decades recall green bean casseroles bound with mushroom soup and topped with crispy fried onions from a can.

Covered dishes, gratins, hot dishes, baked stews, pot pies, pilafs, stratas, scalloped foods—the names alone make your mouth water—all fall under the category of casseroles. What they have in common is that they are baked in a single dish and are served most often as a main course, and sometimes as a side. The word *casserole* also refers to the cookware—often glass, ceramic, or cast-iron—used to cook such food.

It's not hard to figure out why these all-in-one dishes are so popular. They are convenient, easy to assemble, and endlessly versatile, and, more often than not, they can be prepared ahead. Such dishes fit effortlessly into the hectic lives of today's cooks.

For this book, I wanted to update some of those fondly remembered dishes and invent new ones as well. Our culinary landscape has changed over the past few decades. Grocery stores large and small sell dozens of varieties of cheeses, display shelves of artisan breads, and fill produce bins with an array of interesting fruits and vegetables. The meat, poultry, and seafood counters boast far more selections than they did when casseroles first became popular in the mid-twentieth century. This transformation of the marketplace inspires how we all cook, and influenced the choices I made for this collection.

My goal was to use as many fresh ingredients as possible by replacing those omnipresent canned creamed soups (high in sodium) with easily made sauces. In fact, the only soups called for in this collection are low-salt broths. At my farmers' market and in the produce aisles of my local grocery stores, I filled my cart with a cornucopia of seasonal produce for these recipes. Sweet potatoes, chard, fennel, and cauliflower went into cold-weather dishes, while asparagus, sugar snaps, corn, eggplant, and tomatoes were ideal for spring and summer fare. And, yes, you can pour bread crumbs from a can, but by investing only a few extra minutes of time, you can make fresher and far tastier ones.

Casseroles are an American specialty, but countries around the world claim their own one-dish favorites. You'll see Italian roots in Lelia's Venetian Chicken with Porcini Mushrooms and Fontina (page 28), and a French influence in a Provençal Tian of Tomatoes and Summer Squash with Basil and Mint (page 95). Comforting Smoked Sausage, Kale, and Mushroom Cottage Pie (page 116) is reminiscent of English country cooking.

Some of these recipes can be prepped and baked in an hour's time, but others will take the better part of an afternoon and would be perfect to cook on the weekend. A few dishes are best when made and served immediately, while many can be prepared several hours or even a day ahead.

You will find that the casseroles within these pages easily fit into your life—for weeknight suppers, meals for company, for potluck dinners, and as thoughtful gifts for friends or neighbors in need.

When I began the research for this collection, a quick review of many contemporary cookbooks revealed that casseroles were not included. Their indexes went straight from "carrots" to, in some cases, "caviar"! That was my wake-up call to create the recipes in *Sunday Casseroles*. One of my friends put the need for this book very clearly, explaining that in her contemporary plugged-in and harried life, she consistently turns to one-dish meals. They are not supporting players in her culinary repertoire; they have leading roles.

I hope that these special casseroles find a place of honor in your kitchen, and that some day they, too, will evoke warm and wonderful memories. Imagine what Proust would have written, had his mother served him a chicken pot pie!

CASSEROLE TIPS AND GUIDELINES

- Baking dishes with the same volume can vary in their dimensions, which will affect how quickly the ingredients cook. Shallower dishes, for example, tend to cook more quickly than deeper ones. The recipes in this book all call for shallow baking dishes.
- Butter or oil your baking dishes to prevent food from sticking, unless the ingredients are cooked in a generous amount of braising liquid.
- A white sauce (also called béchamel) is often used to bind ingredients in casseroles. To make the sauce, you melt butter, cook a little flour in it, and then add milk, cream, half-and-half (or another liquid) and cook until the mixture thickens. There are two important things to remember: You should cook the flour in the butter for at least 1½ minutes to remove its raw taste, and whisk the sauce constantly once the liquid has been added to prevent the flour from burning on the bottom of the pan.
- Creamy cheeses that melt easily can be used instead of white or cheese sauces. Gorgonzola and mascarpone are good stand-ins.

- After cutting, slicing, or dicing raw meat, poultry, or fish for a casserole, clean the cutting board immediately to prevent contamination. Rinse it under water, and then pour vinegar or squeeze lemon juice over the cutting surface. Finally, wash the board well.
- When cooking pasta for casseroles, use plenty of boiling water (4 to 5 qt/3.8 to 4.7 L per 1 lb/455 g), season generously with salt, and stir during the first few minutes of cooking. Do not add oil to the pasta water or rinse the cooked pasta, both of which will prevent sauces from adhering to pasta.
- When making toasted bread crumbs from scratch for casseroles, choose good-quality artisan-style bread. Sourdough works particularly well, but you can use whole-wheat, multigrain, or rye loaves, too.
- In addition to, or in place of, bread crumbs, try toasted nuts, such as almonds, walnuts, pecans, and peanuts, as toppings to add extra texture and flavor to casseroles.
- To transport a heated casserole, place it in a large roasting pan lined with pot holders or kitchen towels. Cover with foil.

MAKE-AHEAD AND FREEZING GUIDELINES

- To bake a casserole ahead of time, cool completely, and then cover tightly with plastic wrap and refrigerate.
- To freeze a casserole, you can either assemble and freeze or bake and freeze, depending on the recipe. Either way, cool completely and cover tightly with plastic wrap, and then with foil. Add a label with the name of the recipe and the date. Defrost overnight in the refrigerator.

- Whether refrigerated or frozen, bring a casserole to room temperature 30 minutes to 1 hour (but no longer) before baking or reheating. You may need to add extra baking time when a dish has been refrigerated.
- Reheat casseroles in a moderate (around 350°F/180°C) oven, covered, so that they do not dry out on the second go-round. If a casserole seems to be dry, you can stir in a little more of the liquid that was called for in the recipe. Reheating in a microwave will warm the food but will also soften crispy toppings.

SOME BASIC PREPARATIONS

Crème Fraîche

To prepare homemade crème fraîche, whisk 1 cup/240 ml heavy cream and ⅓ cup/75 ml sour cream together in a medium nonreactive bowl. Let stand at room temperature until thickened, about 6 hours. Cover and refrigerate. (Crème fraîche can be stored for up to 1 week, covered, in the refrigerator.) Makes about 1⅓ cups/315 ml.

Crushed Caraway or Fennel Seeds

Coarsely grind caraway or fennel seeds in an electric spice grinder, or place them in a mortar and crush finely with a pestle, or seal them in a plastic bag and pound with a meat mallet or rolling pin. The seeds should be finely crushed.

Toasted Bread Crumbs

Use a one- to two-day-old loaf of good-quality artisan-style country bread with crusts removed. (Sourdough works particularly well, but whole wheat, multigrain, and rye are good, too.) Process enough slices or pieces in a food processor to make 1 cup/55 g of coarse crumbs. Heat 1 tbsp olive oil in a medium, heavy frying pan over medium heat. Add the crumbs and cook, stirring constantly, until they are crisp and rich golden brown, 3 to 4 minutes. You can also use unsalted butter instead of the olive oil. (The bread crumbs can be stored in a plastic self-sealing bag and refrigerated for up to 1 week.) Makes 1 cup/55 g.

Toasted Caraway Seeds

To toast caraway seeds, place them in a small, dry frying pan over medium heat, tossing or stirring lightly until browned and fragrant, 3 to 4 minutes. Watch carefully so they don't burn.

Toasted Nuts

To toast nuts, spread them out on a rimmed baking sheet and place in a preheated 350°F/180°C oven until lightly browned, 5 to 8 minutes. Pecans usually take 5 to 6 minutes, while walnuts and almonds will need 6 to 8 minutes. Watch carefully so they don't burn. Remove from the oven and cool.

CASSEROLE COOKWARE ESSENTIALS

BAKING DISHES

Glass, ceramic, and porcelain dishes do not conduct heat quickly, but they retain it well once a casserole has been baked, so they are popular options. You can use round, oval, square, or rectangular dishes in a variety of sizes. Or you can bake casseroles in small individual dishes. Here's a good basic selection:
- 1½-qt/1.4-L shallow baking dish
- 2-qt/2-L shallow baking dish

- 3-qt/2.8-L shallow baking dish
- 9-by-13-in/23-by-33-cm baking dish
- 4- to 5-qt/3.8- to 4.7-L shallow baking dish
- Set of four 5½-in/14-cm (in diameter) gratin or crème brûlée dishes, to use for individual casseroles
- Set of six 1-cup/240-ml ramekins, for individual pot pies

COOKING EQUIPMENT
- Medium and large saucepans with lids
- Medium (10-in/25-cm) and large (12-in/30.5-cm) frying pans with lids
- Large stockpot with lid
- Rimmed baking sheet

KITCHEN TOOLS AND BOWLS
- Oven thermometer
- Whisks, rubber spatulas, wooden spoons
- 1-, 2-, and 4-cup/240-, 480-, and 960-ml liquid measuring cups
- Set of dry measuring cups
- Measuring spoons
- Tongs
- Citrus zester
- Vegetable peeler
- Box grater
- Set of graduated mixing bowls

KNIVES
- 6- to 8-in/15- to 20-cm chef's knife
- Serrated knife
- 2 paring knives
- 2 or 3 cutting boards

THE CASSEROLE PANTRY

IN THE CUPBOARD
- All-purpose flour
- Broths: reduced-sodium beef and chicken
- Condiments and oils: Dijon mustard, olive and canola oils, cider and balsamic vinegars
- Dried herbs: basil, oregano, rosemary, thyme
- Dried pastas: farfalle, fettuccine, macaroni, penne, rigatoni
- Garlic
- Leftover crusty bread for bread crumbs
- Legumes: canned black beans, cannellini, chickpeas, kidney beans
- Nuts: almonds, peanuts, pecans, walnuts
- Rice: American long-grain, Arborio, basmati, wild
- Spices: cayenne pepper, chili powder, chipotle chile powder, curry powder, fennel seeds, nutmeg, red pepper flakes
- Tomatoes: canned diced tomatoes, tomato paste
- Yellow onions

IN THE FRIDGE
- Cheeses: sharp cheddar, feta, Gruyère, Monterey Jack, Parmesan
- Dairy: butter, cream, crème fraîche, half-and-half, milk, sour cream
- Meats and poultry: andouille sausage, bacon, chorizo, ham, kielbasa, leftover turkey or rotisserie chicken, prosciutto

CHICKEN AND TURKEY FAVORITES

New and Old Traditions

It's no wonder that chicken is such a popular starting point when making a casserole. Is there anything more versatile? You can fashion one-dish meals with cubed or halved breasts, use whole thighs, or shred or slice the meat from a store-bought rotisserie chicken. And turkey is equally adaptable. Turkey cutlets, cubed turkey breasts or tenderloins, ground turkey, and leftovers from the Thanksgiving bird all make excellent primary ingredients for casseroles.

Home cooks often fret that chicken and turkey (no matter the cut) will dry out if included in casseroles, but both hold up beautifully in a hot oven when napped with sauces or covered with vegetables. Morsels of poultry, large or small, consistently come out moist and fork-tender. Some dishes in this chapter will need a short time in the oven while others will require a longer stay. In Lelia's Venetian Chicken with Porcini Mushrooms and Fontina (page 28), sliced chicken breasts coated with mushroom sauce are meltingly tender in less than thirty minutes. But for Baked Chicken, Fennel, and Tomatoes (page 20), count on an hour and a half before the chicken thighs are tender and their meat is falling off the bone.

In many recipes, chicken and turkey are interchangeable. Creamed Turkey, Fall Vegetables, and Wild Rice Bake (page 30) can easily be prepared with chicken, and for Turkey Cutlets Baked with Gruyère and Onions (page 36), chicken yields equally delicious results.

You'll find old favorites with new twists, such as Chicken, Baby Limas, and Corn with Parmesan Rice (page 25)—a riff on succotash—as well as inventive new creations, such as Turkey with Red and Green Grapes on Walnut Polenta (page 33). I think you'll find them all tempting—poultry perfection in one dish.

Chicken, Sweet Potato, and Bacon Casserole

This casserole is perfect for fall, when supermarket display bins are overflowing with copper-fleshed sweet potatoes. If you've never used this versatile tuber in a casserole, you'll be surprised by how much flavor, not to mention color, it will add. In this recipe, sautéed chicken breasts seasoned with sage and thyme are covered with pan-fried sweet potatoes, onion, and bacon, and then coated with a creamy white sauce. The chicken and potatoes, as well as the sauce, can be cooked ahead, so there's no last-minute angst.

Serves 4

PREP TIME:
20 minutes

START-TO-FINISH TIME:
1 hour, 20 minutes

MAKE AHEAD:
Yes

4 boneless, skinless chicken breast halves
  (about 8 oz/225 g each)

1 tbsp dried thyme

1½ tsp dried sage

Kosher salt

1 tsp freshly ground black pepper

12 oz/340 g sweet potatoes
  (see Market Note)

1 medium red onion

5 tbsp/75 ml olive oil

½ cup/120 ml reduced-sodium chicken broth

¼ cup/60 ml dry white wine

5 slices good-quality smoked bacon

1 tbsp unsalted butter

1 tbsp all-purpose flour

1 cup/240 ml whole milk

⅓ cup/30 g grated Gruyère cheese

Fresh sage sprigs for garnish (optional)

Fresh thyme sprigs for garnish (optional)

1. Arrange a rack in the middle of the oven and preheat to 350°F/180°C. Generously butter a 9-by-13-in/23-by-33-cm or another shallow 3-qt/2.8-L baking dish.

2. Pat the chicken dry with paper towels. Place a chicken breast on a work surface and, with a sharp knife held parallel with the surface, cut the breast in half horizontally. Repeat with the remaining breasts. You will have 8 chicken pieces. In a small bowl, mix together the thyme, sage, 1 tsp salt, and the pepper. Set aside 1 tsp of this seasoning. Season both sides of each piece of the chicken with the remaining mixture.

3. Peel the sweet potatoes and cut into ¼-in-/6-mm-thick rounds. Stack several rounds on top of each other and cut into ¼-in-/6-mm-wide strips. Peel the onion, halve through the root end, and slice into ¼-in-/6-mm-wide strips.

4. Heat 3 tbsp of the olive oil until hot in a large frying pan over medium heat. Add the chicken breasts and sauté until lightly browned, 2 to 3 minutes per side. Remove the chicken to the prepared baking dish. Add the chicken broth and wine to the pan and whisk to scrape up any browned bits on the bottom. Cook, stirring, until the liquid has reduced to ¼ cup/60 ml, 3 to 4 minutes. Pour over the chicken breasts.

5. In the same frying pan set over medium heat, fry the bacon until crisp, 4 to 5 minutes. Drain on paper towels and, when cool, chop coarsely. Discard all but 1 tbsp of the drippings in the pan and add the remaining 2 tbsp olive oil. Set the frying pan over medium heat, and when hot, add the sweet potatoes and onion and sauté, stirring, until softened, 7 to 8 minutes. Season the vegetables with salt and spoon them over the chicken. Sprinkle with the bacon. (The casserole can be prepared up to this point 1 day ahead. Cool, cover, and refrigerate. Bring to room temperature for 30 minutes before proceeding.)

6. Melt the butter until hot in a medium saucepan over medium heat. Add the flour and cook, stirring constantly, for 1½ to 2 minutes. Gradually whisk in the milk and the reserved 1 tsp of seasoning. Bring the mixture to a gentle boil, whisking constantly, and cook until it thickens enough to coat the back of a spoon, about 3 minutes. Taste the sauce and season with salt if needed. (The sauce can be prepared 1 day ahead; cool, cover, and refrigerate separately from the baking dish. Gently reheat over low temperature.) Drizzle the sauce over the ingredients in the casserole and sprinkle with the Gruyère. Cover the casserole loosely with a sheet of foil.

7. Bake the casserole until the chicken is cooked through and tender, about 20 minutes. Remove from the oven and cool the casserole for 5 minutes.

8. If desired, garnish the center of the dish with some sage and thyme sprigs before serving.

 MARKET NOTE:

Two types of sweet potato are available in the United States. One has pale tan skin and light orange flesh, while the other (often erroneously labeled "yam" in the supermarket) has a darker skin and rich, copper-hued flesh. The latter variety (with its bright orange flesh) is the one I like to use in this recipe.

Baked Chicken, Fennel, and Tomatoes

Humble chicken thighs are magically transformed into a delicious, fork-tender entrée when baked slowly in a casserole with vegetables. These herb-scented thighs are combined with carrots, fennel, and tomatoes, and then simmered in a flavorful mixture of broth, wine, and orange juice. Don't be put off by the long list of ingredients, because once this dish is assembled, it goes in the oven to bake, totally unattended. A definite crowd-pleaser, this casserole can be prepared two days ahead and will actually improve in flavor. Ladle this delicious mélange into shallow bowls to serve alone, or spoon it over mounds of fettuccine. Add an arugula salad and a warm baguette, and you have yourself a meal.

Serves 4 to 8

PREP TIME:
30 minutes

START-TO-FINISH TIME:
2 hours

MAKE AHEAD:
Yes

FREEZE:
Yes, after baking (see directions on page 11)

8 bone-in chicken thighs (2½ to 3 lb/1.2 to 1.4 kg total), trimmed of fat and any dangling skin

1 tbsp dried basil

2 tsp dried oregano

Kosher salt

½ tsp freshly ground black pepper

3 tbsp olive oil, plus more if needed

1½ cups/190 g chopped onion

1½ cups/200 g diagonally sliced carrots (¼ in/6 mm thick)

2 medium fennel bulbs (1½ to 2 lb/680 to 910 g total), trimmed, halved, cored, and cut into ½-in-/12-mm-thick wedges

1 tsp fennel seeds, crushed (see page 12)

Scant ½ tsp red pepper flakes

3 cups/720 ml reduced-sodium chicken broth

1 cup/240 ml orange juice

2 strips orange zest (each about 4 in/10 cm long and ½ in/12 mm wide), plus 1 tbsp finely julienned orange zest (optional) for garnish

1. Arrange a rack in the middle of the oven and preheat to 350°F/180°C. Have ready a large shallow 4- to 5-qt/3.8- to 4.7-L baking dish.

2. Pat the chicken dry with paper towels. Combine the basil, oregano, 1 tsp salt, and the pepper in a small bowl. Season both sides of each chicken thigh with this mixture.

3. Heat the olive oil in a large, heavy, deep-sided frying pan over medium-high heat until hot. Add several thighs without crowding the pan, skin-side down, and brown on both sides, 8 to 10 minutes total. Remove to the baking dish and repeat with the remaining thighs.

4. Add the onion, carrots, and fennel to the frying pan, using more oil if needed. Cook, stirring until the vegetables have softened slightly, 8 to 10 minutes. Sprinkle the fennel seeds and red pepper flakes over the mixture. Add the chicken broth, orange juice, the 2 orange zest strips, wine, and tomatoes and bring the mixture to a simmer.

5. In a small bowl, use a fork to blend the flour and butter into a smooth paste and whisk it into the simmering liquid, a little at a time, to thicken slightly. Season with more salt if needed. Ladle the mixture over the chicken in the baking dish.

6. Bake, uncovered, until the chicken is very tender when pierced with a sharp knife and the liquid has reduced and thickened somewhat, for 1 hour and 30 to 45 minutes. (The casserole can be baked 1 day ahead. Cool, cover, and refrigerate. Reheat in a preheated 350°F/180°C oven until hot, 30 to 40 minutes.) Discard the orange strips.

7. To serve, spoon into shallow bowls and, if desired, garnish with some julienned orange zest. Pass the Parmesan cheese for sprinkling.

½ cup/120 ml dry white wine

One 28-oz/800-g can diced tomatoes, drained well

3 tbsp all-purpose flour

2 tbsp unsalted butter, at room temperature

½ cup/60 g grated Parmesan cheese, preferably Parmigiano-Reggiano

Cornmeal-Coated Chicken with Ancho Chiles, Beans, and Corn

My mother rarely used chile peppers of any variety. She added chili powder to her spaghetti sauce, and stuffed and baked green bell peppers, but that was the extent of her "chile" repertoire. I have countless choices when it comes to chiles. My local markets boast an array of hot, mild, fresh, and dried ones. Ancho chiles (deep rust–hued dried poblanos) are mild and even fruity in taste, and give this earthy casserole an extra depth of flavor.

Serves 6

PREP TIME:
35 minutes

START-TO-FINISH TIME:
1 hour, 50 minutes

MAKE AHEAD:
Yes

FREEZE:
Yes, after baking (see directions on page 11)

2 ancho chiles (about ¾ oz/20 g total; see Market Note)

Kosher salt

Freshly ground black pepper

1 tsp ground cumin

6 bone-in chicken thighs (about 3 lb/1.4 kg total), trimmed of excess fat and dangling skin

½ cup/60 g all-purpose flour

¾ cup/105 g yellow cornmeal

2 large eggs

⅓ cup/75 ml vegetable oil

2 cups/480 ml reduced-sodium chicken broth

One 28-oz/800-g can diced tomatoes, with their juices

4 garlic cloves, peeled and crushed

1 tbsp dried oregano

One 15-oz/430-g can black beans, rinsed and drained

1½ cups/260 g fresh corn kernels (about 3 ears)

Crushed tortilla chips

Grated sharp white cheddar or Monterey Jack cheese

Lime wedges

Chopped fresh cilantro

1. Arrange a rack in the middle of the oven and preheat to 350°F/180°C.

2. Put the chiles in a small bowl and cover with ¾ cup/180 ml boiling water. Let sit for 15 minutes, or until the chiles are soft. Drain well. Then, wearing rubber gloves, slit the chiles and scrape out and discard the seeds. Coarsely chop the chiles, measure 2 tbsp, and set aside. (Save any extra for another use.)

3. Combine 1 tsp salt, ½ tsp black pepper, and ½ tsp of the cumin in a small bowl. Season the chicken thighs on both sides with this mixture. Spread the flour on a dinner plate and the cornmeal on another. Whisk the eggs in a shallow bowl to blend well. Dredge each thigh in flour, then dip in the eggs, and finally dredge in the cornmeal.

4. Heat the vegetable oil in large, heavy, ovenproof frying pan over medium heat until very hot. Add the thighs to the pan in a single layer, in batches if necessary. (The oil should be hot enough that it sizzles when the chicken is added.) Sauté the thighs until golden brown, 3 to 4 minutes per side. Remove the chicken to a plate, and pour off any remaining oil in the pan.

continued . . .

5. To the same frying pan, add the chicken broth, tomatoes, garlic, oregano, remaining ½ tsp cumin, ½ tsp salt, and the reserved 2 tbsp chopped ancho chiles. Stir in the black beans and corn and bring the mixture to a simmer. Taste and season with more salt and pepper if needed. Return the chicken to the frying pan, and then carefully transfer to the oven.

6. Bake, uncovered, for 20 minutes. Turn the chicken and cook until the thighs are very tender when pierced with a sharp knife and most of the liquids have evaporated, 30 to 40 minutes more. (The casserole can be prepared 1 day ahead; cool, cover, and refrigerate. Reheat in a preheated 350°F/180°C oven until hot, 30 to 40 minutes.)

7. Serve the chicken and vegetables straight from the frying pan, accompanied by bowls of crushed tortilla chips, grated cheese, lime wedges, and chopped cilantro.

 MARKET NOTE:

Ancho chiles (dried poblanos) are available at many grocery stores (sometimes in the produce area), and in specialty food shops.

Chicken, Baby Limas, and Corn with Parmesan Rice

This dish, which is redolent of succotash, is easy to make when you have leftover chicken or just want to use a rotisserie bird from the supermarket more imaginatively. Diced chicken is paired with sautéed corn, baby limas, onions, and rice, and then baked in a mixture of broth and wine. Lemon zest provides a refreshing note to this homey casserole, while Parmesan offers a creamy accent.

Serves 4

PREP TIME:
30 minutes

START-TO-FINISH TIME:
1 hour, 25 minutes

MAKE AHEAD
No

3 thick slices bacon

1½ tsp olive oil

½ cup/65 g chopped onion

1 cup/150 g fresh corn kernels (about 2 ears)

1 cup/170 g frozen baby lima beans, defrosted and patted dry

1½ tsp dried thyme

1 tsp kosher salt

⅜ tsp freshly ground black pepper

2 cups/280 g diced cooked chicken (¾-in/2-cm dice)

1 cup/215 g long-grain rice, preferably basmati

2½ cups/600 ml reduced-sodium chicken broth

¼ cup/60 ml white wine

¼ cup/10 g chopped fresh flat-leaf parsley

1½ tsp grated lemon zest

1½ tbsp unsalted butter, cut into small pieces

½ cup/60 g grated Parmesan cheese, preferably Parmigiano-Reggiano

1. Arrange a rack in the middle of the oven and preheat to 350°F/180°C. Generously butter a 2-qt/2-L shallow baking dish.

2. Fry the bacon until crisp in a medium frying pan over medium heat. Drain on paper towels, coarsely chop, and set aside. Pour off all but 1½ tsp of the drippings in the pan and add the olive oil. Heat over medium heat, add the onion, and sauté, stirring, until softened, 3 to 4 minutes. Add the corn and lima beans and cook, stirring, 3 minutes more. Remove from the heat and stir in the thyme, salt, and pepper.

3. Put the chicken, vegetable mixture, rice, chicken broth, wine, 2 tbsp of the parsley, and the lemon zest in the prepared baking dish. Stir to combine well. Dot the top of the casserole with the butter pieces. Cover the casserole tightly with foil and bake until the rice is cooked and has absorbed all the liquid, 40 to 45 minutes.

4. While the casserole is in the oven, combine the bacon with the remaining 2 tbsp parsley.

5. When the casserole is done, remove the foil and stir in the Parmesan cheese. Sprinkle the top of the casserole with the parsley and bacon before serving.

Lelia's Venetian Chicken with Porcini Mushrooms and Fontina

During a trip to Italy with food-loving friends, my fellow travelers and I arranged to take a cooking lesson with Lelia Passi, a vivacious Italian who just happened to live in a beautiful palazzo overlooking Venice's Grand Canal. In spite of her gorgeous surroundings, our host was unpretentious and down to earth—just like her food. She shepherded us into her kitchen, where we assembled a dinner that included chicken breasts topped with fontina and prosciutto, baked under a creamy porcini mushroom sauce. This talented teacher added a hint of curry powder as a subtle seasoning to the dish. She encouraged us to assemble the casserole completely and let it rest before baking, so that all the delectable flavors would have a chance to meld. On my side of the Atlantic, I like to serve this dish with a purée of butternut squash and a green salad sprinkled with toasted walnuts and dried cherries.

Serves 4 to 8

PREP TIME:
25 minutes

START-TO-FINISH TIME:
2 hours, 25 minutes (including 1 hour for the casserole to rest at room temperature)

MAKE AHEAD:
Yes

2 oz/55 g dried porcini mushrooms

4 boneless, skinless chicken breast halves (about 8 oz/225 g each)

2 tsp curry powder

¼ cup/60 ml olive oil

Kosher salt

Freshly ground black pepper

2 tbsp unsalted butter

8 oz/225 g brown mushrooms (cremini), cleaned and thinly sliced lengthwise through the caps and stems

½ cup/120 ml dry sherry or dry Marsala

1⅓ cups/240 ml heavy or whipping cream

8 thin slices prosciutto

1 cup/120 g grated Italian fontina cheese (see Market Note)

2 tbsp chopped fresh flat-leaf parsley

1. Generously butter a 9-by-13-in/23-by-33-cm or another shallow 3-qt/2.8-L baking dish.

2. Put the porcini mushrooms in a strainer and rinse under running water to remove any grit. Then put them in a medium bowl and cover with 2 cups/480 ml boiling water. Let stand until softened, 15 to 20 minutes. Strain the mushrooms and soaking liquid over a bowl through a strainer lined with a paper towel, pressing down on the mushrooms with a spoon to extract as much liquid as possible. Reserve the soaking liquid. Coarsely chop the porcini and set aside.

3. Place a chicken breast on a work surface and, with a sharp knife held parallel with the surface, cut the breast in half horizontally. Repeat with the remaining breasts. You will have eight chicken pieces. In a shallow dish, whisk the curry powder and olive oil together. Dip each breast into the oil and coat well on both sides.

4. Place a heavy, large frying pan over medium-high heat. When hot, add as many chicken breasts as will fit comfortably in a single layer. Cook until lightly browned on both sides, turning several times, 5 to 6 minutes total. Remove the cooked chicken to the baking dish, and arrange in a single layer. Continue until all the chicken has been sautéed. Season the chicken with salt and pepper.

5. Melt the butter in a medium frying pan over medium-high heat. When hot, add the sliced brown mushrooms and cook, stirring occasionally, until browned and no liquid remains, 5 minutes or more. Season with ¾ tsp salt and several grinds of pepper. Add 2 tbsp of the sherry to the pan. Cook until all the liquid has evaporated, about 1 minute. Add the reserved porcini, 1 cup/240 ml of the reserved soaking liquid, the cream, and the remaining sherry. Cook, stirring, until the sauce thickens very slightly, about 5 minutes.

6. Top each chicken breast with a slice of prosciutto, cut to fit. (You may have some prosciutto left over.) Sprinkle an equal amount of fontina cheese over each prosciutto-covered breast. Pour the sauce over the chicken. Cover with plastic wrap and leave at cool room temperature for 1 hour to develop the flavors. (To make the casserole a day ahead, cover and refrigerate the chicken, omitting the resting time. Bring to room temperature for 30 minutes, and continue with the recipe.)

7. Arrange a rack in the middle of the oven and preheat to 400°F/200°C. Bake, uncovered, until the cheese has melted and the chicken is hot all the way through, about 20 minutes. Remove from the oven and sprinkle with the parsley before serving.

 MARKET NOTE:

Buy good-quality Italian fontina, rather than Danish, for this recipe.

Creamed Turkey, Fall Vegetables, and Wild Rice Bake

Although I adore preparing the annual turkey for my family on Thanksgiving Day, I look forward even more to dishes made with the leftover bird. Memories of my mother's delectable creamed turkey and vegetables served over rice at post-Thanksgiving meals inspired this casserole. A classic cheese sauce seasoned with curry powder is combined with diced turkey and a medley of sautéed vegetables, along with both wild and white rice. Baked until piping hot, this striking mixture is then sprinkled with golden raisins and pecans.

Serves 4

PREP TIME:
1 hour, including cooking the rice

START-TO-FINISH TIME:
2 hours

MAKE AHEAD:
Yes

3 tbsp unsalted butter

3 medium carrots, peeled and cut into ½-in/12-mm dice

3 medium parsnips, peeled and cut into ½-in/12-mm dice

1 large fennel bulb, trimmed, cored, and chopped

¾ cup/85 g chopped leeks (white and light green parts only)

2 cups/280 g cooked diced turkey (½-in/12-mm dice)

2 cups/300 g cooked wild rice (see Cooking Tip)

1 cup/195 g cooked long-grain white rice, preferably basmati

1. Arrange a rack in the middle of the oven and preheat to 350°F/180°C. Butter a shallow 2-qt/2-L baking dish.

2. Melt the butter until hot in a large, heavy frying pan over medium-high heat. Add the carrots, parsnips, fennel, and leeks and cook, stirring, until softened, about 15 minutes. Remove from the heat and stir in the turkey and both the wild and white rice.

3. For the Curried Cheddar Sauce: Melt the butter until hot in a medium saucepan over medium heat. Add the flour and cook, stirring constantly, for 1½ to 2 minutes. Pour in the half-and-half and chicken broth and bring to a gentle boil, whisking constantly until the mixture thickens enough to coat the back of a spoon, 3 to 4 minutes. Stir in the cheddar, curry powder, ¾ tsp salt, and cayenne. Taste and season with more salt if needed.

4. Pour the sauce over the mixture in the frying pan and stir well to combine. Season with salt if needed. Spread the mixture evenly in the prepared baking dish. (The casserole can be prepared up to this point 1 day ahead. Cool, cover, and refrigerate. Bring to room temperature 30 minutes before baking.)

5. Bake the casserole, uncovered, until hot, about 25 minutes. Combine the pecans and raisins and sprinkle them on top of the casserole; bake for 5 minutes more. Remove from the oven and sprinkle the casserole with the parsley before serving.

Curried Cheddar Sauce

3 tbsp unsalted butter

3½ tbsp/25 g all-purpose flour

1½ cups/360 ml half-and-half

1½ cups/360 ml reduced-sodium chicken or turkey broth

½ cup/50 g grated sharp white cheddar cheese

1 tbsp plus 1 tsp curry powder

Kosher salt

Pinch of cayenne pepper

½ cup/55 g pecans, toasted and coarsely chopped (see page 12)

½ cup/85 g golden raisins, soaked in 1 cup/ 240 ml hot water for 5 minutes and drained

2 tbsp chopped fresh flat-leaf parsley

COOKING TIP:

To cook wild rice, add 1 cup/215 g wild rice to a saucepan filled with 8 cups/2 L of boiling water and cook, uncovered, for 45 minutes. The rice will double in size and still be somewhat crunchy when done. Remove from the heat and drain through a strainer.

Turkey and Corn Tortilla Casserole with Lime-Scented Sour Cream

The spicy chili in this casserole is prepared with ground turkey, a lighter alternative to more traditional beef or pork. This chili is layered with corn tortillas and sour cream, and accented with lime and cilantro. When baked, the tortillas soften, melding into the mixture, almost like tamales.

Serves 6

PREP TIME:
30 minutes

START-TO-FINISH TIME:
1 hour, 30 minutes

MAKE AHEAD:
Yes

2 tbsp olive oil

2 cups/250 g chopped onion

1 cup/130 g chopped red bell pepper

2 tsp chopped garlic

2 lb/910 g ground turkey, preferably half dark (thigh meat) and half white (breast meat)

1 tbsp plus 1 tsp chili powder

1 tbsp plus 1 tsp ground cumin

1 tbsp plus 1 tsp dried oregano

Kosher salt

1 tsp chipotle chile powder

One 15-oz/430-g can diced tomatoes, drained

1 cup/240 ml reduced-sodium chicken broth

One 4½-oz/130-g can green chiles, drained

2 cups/480 ml sour cream

2 cups/240 g grated Monterey Jack cheese

¼ cup plus 2 tbsp/15 g chopped fresh cilantro

2 tsp grated lime zest

Eight 6-in/15-cm corn tortillas, cut into quarters

1. Arrange a rack in the middle of the oven and preheat to 375°F/190°C. Oil a 9-by-13-in/23-by-33-cm or another shallow 3-qt/2.8-L baking dish.

2. Heat the olive oil in a large, heavy frying pan set over medium heat. When hot, add the onion, bell pepper, and garlic and cook, stirring, for 4 to 5 minutes to soften the vegetables. Add the ground turkey, chili powder, cumin, oregano, 2 tsp salt, and the chipotle chile powder. Cook, stirring often to break up any lumps, until the turkey has cooked through, about 6 minutes.

3. Add the tomatoes, chicken broth, and green chiles and cook, stirring, until all liquids have evaporated, 15 to 20 minutes. Taste and season with more salt if needed.

4. In a medium bowl, whisk together the sour cream, 1 cup/ 120 g of the Monterey Jack, the cilantro, and lime zest.

5. Spread one-third of the turkey mixture in the baking dish. Arrange half of the tortilla quarters over the mixture, and then spread one-third of the sour cream mixture over the tortillas. Repeat to make another layer. Layer the remaining turkey mixture on top, cover with the remaining sour cream mixture, and sprinkle with the remaining Monterey Jack. (The casserole can be prepared up to this point 2 hours ahead; cover and refrigerate. Bring to room temperature 30 minutes to 1 hour before baking.)

6. Bake, uncovered, until the casserole is hot and the cheese has melted, 25 to 30 minutes. Serve immediately.

Turkey with Red and Green Grapes on Walnut Polenta

Grapes, walnuts, and turkey are all reminiscent of fall, especially when brought together, as they are in this beautiful harvest casserole. A layer of polenta, scented with toasted walnuts and fresh rosemary, is topped with cubed and seared turkey tenderloins, and then covered with a rich, dark sauce prepared with balsamic vinegar, honey, and grapes. In both looks and taste, this is a striking dish; yet it is easy to assemble and also inexpensive. Add a loaf of warm ciabatta bread and a salad of baby romaine tossed in a lemon dressing to complete the meal.

Serves 5 to 6

PREP TIME:
15 minutes

START-TO-FINISH TIME:
1 hour, 10 minutes

MAKE AHEAD:
Yes, partially

Walnut Polenta

3 cups/720 ml reduced-sodium chicken broth

1 cup/140 g yellow cornmeal

2 tbsp unsalted butter

1 cup plus 2 tbsp/90 g grated Gruyère cheese

½ cup/55 g walnuts, toasted (see page 12)
  and very finely chopped

2¼ tsp chopped fresh rosemary

Kosher salt

2 tsp crushed dried rosemary
  (see Market Note)

¾ tsp kosher salt

¾ tsp freshly ground black pepper

1 lb/455 g turkey tenderloins, cut into
  1-in/2.5-cm cubes (see Market Note)

2 tbsp olive oil

¾ cup/180 ml reduced-sodium chicken broth

¼ cup plus 2 tbsp/90 ml balsamic vinegar

3 tbsp honey

¾ tsp cornstarch

¾ cup/130 g red seedless grapes

¾ cup/130 g green seedless grapes

3 or 4 fresh rosemary sprigs for garnish

1. Arrange a rack in the middle of the oven and preheat to 350°F/180°C. Generously butter a 9-by-13-in/23-by-33-cm or another shallow 3-qt/2.8-L baking dish.

2. For the Walnut Polenta: Pour the chicken broth into a medium, heavy saucepan over medium-high heat and bring to a boil. Whisk in the cornmeal, a little at a time, in a fine stream. Continue whisking constantly until the mixture thickens and starts to pull away from the sides of the pan, about 5 minutes. Remove from the heat and whisk in the butter until melted. Gradually whisk in the Gruyère until it has melted. Stir in the chopped walnuts and rosemary. Taste and add salt if needed.

3. Immediately pour the mixture into the prepared casserole and, using a metal spatula or table knife, spread evenly. The polenta will be quite stiff. (The polenta can be prepared 1 day ahead; cool, cover with plastic wrap, and refrigerate. Bring to room temperature 1 hour before continuing with the recipe.)

4. Combine the dried rosemary, salt, and pepper in a medium mixing bowl and stir to blend. Pat the turkey cubes dry, add them to the bowl, and toss well to coat with the seasonings.

continued . . .

5. Add the olive oil to a large, heavy frying pan over medium-high heat and, when the oil is very hot but not smoking, add the turkey. Cook, turning frequently, until the turkey is seared on all sides and very lightly browned, only 2 to 2½ minutes. Remove to a platter.

6. Add the chicken broth to the same frying pan over medium-high heat and, using a whisk, deglaze the pan by scraping any browned bits on the bottom into the broth. Add the balsamic vinegar and honey and cook, stirring, until the mixture has reduced by half, 5 minutes or longer. In a small bowl, mix the cornstarch with ¾ tsp cold water until smooth, and then whisk into the sauce in the frying pan. Cook, whisking, until the sauce thickens. Add the grapes to the frying pan, along with any juices that have collected on the platter with the turkey. Scatter the turkey over the polenta, and then spoon the sauce and grapes over the turkey.

7. Bake, uncovered, until the polenta is hot and the turkey cubes are cooked through, about 20 minutes. Garnish the center of the casserole with the rosemary sprigs before serving.

 MARKET NOTE:

Crushed rosemary can be found with other herbs and spices in most supermarkets.

Turkey tenderloins are available in many supermarkets and generally weigh between 10 and 12 oz/280 to 340 g. As their name implies, they are extra tender, but they are not expensive. If unavailable, you can substitute boneless turkey breast.

Turkey Cutlets Baked with Gruyère and Onions

Because this casserole is easy to assemble and needs less than half an hour in the oven, it's perfect for a weeknight meal. The recipe is based on a French dish of baked veal scallops and onions that I made for many years. One day, on a whim, I tried turkey cutlets instead of costly veal and loved the results. Quickly sautéed onions are spread in a baking dish, topped with thin turkey cutlets seasoned with lemon and fresh thyme, and finished with more onions and a topping of bread crumbs and Gruyère. A salad of baby spinach and sliced Belgian endive tossed with a mustard-scented vinaigrette would make a good accompaniment.

Serves 4

PREP TIME:
15 minutes

START-TO-FINISH TIME:
1 hour

MAKE AHEAD:
Yes

2 tbsp unsalted butter

2 cups/250 g halved and thinly sliced onions

2 tsp minced garlic

1 lb/455 g turkey breast cutlets, cut about ¼ in/6 mm thick (see Market Note)

1 tsp kosher salt

¼ tsp freshly ground black pepper

1 tbsp fresh lemon juice

1 tsp grated lemon zest

2½ tbsp chopped fresh thyme, plus a few sprigs for garnish

½ cup/120 ml dry white wine

¼ cup plus 2 tbsp/90 ml reduced-sodium chicken broth

¾ cup/60 g grated Gruyère cheese

½ cup/30 g Toasted Bread Crumbs (page 12), made with butter

1. Arrange a rack in the middle of the oven and preheat to 350°F/180°C. Generously butter a shallow 2-qt/2-L baking dish.

2. Melt the butter in a medium, heavy frying pan over medium heat. When hot, add the onions and sauté, stirring constantly, until translucent and very lightly browned, 4 to 5 minutes. Add the garlic and cook, stirring, 1 minute more. Remove the onions and garlic to a plate.

3. Place a turkey cutlet between two sheets of waxed paper and, using a meat pounder or rolling pin, pound the meat until it is ⅛ in/3 mm thick. Repeat with the remaining cutlets. Combine the salt and pepper in a small bowl and season the turkey cutlets on both sides.

4. Spread half of the onions in the baking dish. Arrange the cutlets in a single overlapping layer on top. Drizzle the cutlets with the lemon juice and sprinkle with the lemon zest and 2 tbsp of the chopped thyme. Spread the remaining onions over the turkey. Combine the wine and chicken broth in a small bowl and pour evenly over the turkey. (The casserole can be prepared up to this point 2 hours ahead; cool, cover, and refrigerate. Bring to room temperature 30 minutes before continuing with the recipe.)

5. When ready to bake, stir the Gruyère and bread crumbs together in a small bowl and sprinkle over the top of the casserole. Bake, uncovered, until the topping is crisp, the cheese has melted, and the turkey is tender when pierced with a knife, about 20 minutes. (There will still be some liquid in the casserole when the dish is finished; that is okay.) Remove from the oven and cool for 5 minutes. Sprinkle the casserole with the remaining 1½ tsp chopped thyme and garnish the center with a few thyme sprigs before serving.

 MARKET NOTE:

Turkey cutlets are available in some supermarkets. If you can't find them, ask the butcher to cut ¼-in-/6-mm-thick slices from a boneless turkey breast.

ALL MANNER OF MEATS

Hearty Casseroles, Warm and Satisfying

This chapter presents hearty recipes for casseroles that are made with beef, veal, pork, and lamb. They are perfect for chilly days or cold nights, when you have a robust appetite and are craving rich and satisfying fare.

The inspiration for these dishes came from cuisines around the world, as well as from traditional American fare. Both Provençal Daube de Boeuf with Olives, Tomatoes, and Orange (page 42) and Cassoulet Rapide (page 53) have French origins and deliver big, bold flavors. Baked Veal Shanks alla Primavera (page 46) are inspired by Italy's celebrated osso buco. Closer to home, Corned Beef and Cabbage with Country Mustard Sauce (page 44) and Cider-Baked Pork, Red Cabbage, and Apples (page 55) suggest New England, where I live. Both are remarkably filling, and need only a warm loaf of dark bread and a simple salad to complete the meal.

Many of these casseroles have the additional convenience of improving in flavor when made ahead. The daube, cassoulet, and veal shanks can be prepared a day or two in advance, and will taste even better after their flavors have had a chance to meld. They freeze beautifully, too.

So when the weather team predicts yet another week of frosty temperatures, make one of these recipes to bring plenty of warmth to your table.

Provençal Daube de Boeuf with Olives, Tomatoes, and Orange

Daube de boeuf à la provençale is a classic French stew of beef and vegetables braised in red wine and broth, accented by olives, tomatoes, and orange zest. Typically, the beef is marinated a day ahead, then cooked in a deep-sided, covered casserole called a *daubière*, from which the word *daube* is derived. For my version, I omit the marinade and bake the stew, uncovered, in a shallow baking dish. After a couple of hours in the oven, the beef cubes are fork-tender and the cooking liquids have cooked down to a thick, rich sauce. This robust all-in-one-dish main with vibrant flavors is delicious served with sautéed polenta slices and a warm baguette for sopping up the delectable sauce.

Serves 6

PREP TIME:
30 minutes

START-TO-FINISH TIME:
3 hours

MAKE AHEAD:
Yes

FREEZE:
Yes, after baking (see directions on page 11)

Daube de Boeuf

½ cup/60 g all-purpose flour

1 tbsp herbes de Provence (see Market Note)

Kosher salt

½ tsp coarsely ground black pepper

3 lb/1.4 kg beef stew meat (such as boneless chuck), cut into 1½- to 2-in/4- to 5-cm chunks, trimmed of excess fat

¼ cup/60 ml olive oil, plus more if needed

1½ cups/190 g coarsely chopped onions

8 oz/225 g carrots, peeled and cut on the diagonal into ¼-in-/6-mm-thick slices

1 tbsp chopped garlic

1 tbsp tomato paste

2½ cups/600 ml reduced-sodium beef broth

1½ cups/360 ml dry red wine

3 strips orange zest, each about 3 in/7.5 cm long and 1 in/2.5 cm wide

½ cup/75 g pitted French or Italian green olives, such as Lucques, Picholine, or Castelvetrano, left whole or halved

½ cup/75 g pitted Kalamata olives, left whole or halved

1. Arrange a rack in the middle of the oven and preheat to 350°F/180°C. Have ready a 9-by-13-in/23-by-33-cm baking dish.

2. For the Daube de Boeuf: Mix together ¼ cup/30 g of the flour, the herbes de Provence, 2 tsp salt, and the pepper in a small bowl and spread on a dinner plate. Pat the beef dry and dredge in the seasoned flour mixture, reserving any of the remaining seasoned flour.

3. Heat the olive oil in a large, heavy, deep-sided frying pan over medium heat until hot. Add enough beef to fit comfortably in a single layer, and sauté, turning, until browned on all sides, 5 to 6 minutes. Remove with a slotted spoon to a large plate. Repeat, adding more oil if needed, until all the beef has been browned.

4. If there is not enough oil in the pan after browning the meat, add 1 to 2 tbsp more and heat over medium heat until hot. Add the onions and carrots and sauté until the onions are lightly browned and the carrots are slightly tender, 3 to 4 minutes. Add the chopped garlic and tomato paste and cook, stirring, for 30 seconds more. Return the meat to the pan and sprinkle with any leftover seasoned flour and the remaining ¼ cup/30 g of unseasoned flour.

Toss and cook, stirring, for 1 minute. Stir in the beef broth, wine, and orange zest and bring the mixture to a simmer.

5. Ladle the beef and vegetable mixture into the baking dish, and bake, uncovered, for 45 minutes. Stir in all the olives and the tomatoes and continue to bake until the meat is tender when pierced with a knife and the liquid has reduced and thickened, about 1 hour and 20 minutes. (The cooking time can vary, so watch carefully after 1 hour.) Taste and season with more salt if needed. Remove and discard the orange zest. Cover loosely with foil while you prepare the polenta. (The daube can be prepared 2 days ahead; cool, cover, and refrigerate. Reheat in a preheated 350°F/180°C oven, adding extra broth and wine in equal amounts if too thick, until hot, 30 to 40 minutes.)

6. For the polenta: Heat enough olive oil to cover the bottom of a large, heavy frying pan in a thin layer. Place over medium heat and when hot, add enough polenta rounds to fit comfortably in a single layer. Sauté until lightly browned, at least 2 minutes per side. Repeat with the remaining rounds.

7. To serve, arrange three polenta rounds in each of six shallow bowls. Ladle the beef and vegetables over them and sprinkle with parsley.

One 15-oz/430-g can diced tomatoes, drained well, or 12 oz/340 g plum or Campari tomatoes, halved, seeded, and cut into 1-in/2.5-cm pieces

Polenta

Olive oil for sautéing

One 1- to 1⅛-lb/455- to 510-g roll of pre-cooked polenta, cut into ½-in/12-mm rounds (see Market Note)

2 tbsp chopped fresh flat-leaf parsley

 MARKET NOTE:

Herbes de Provence, a blend of dried herbs often used in Provençal cooking, is available in many supermarkets. If you can't find it, you can make your own mix. Stir together 2 tbsp dried thyme leaves, 2 tsp dried oregano, 1 tsp dried summer savory, and 1 tsp dried marjoram. Store at room temperature in an airtight jar.

Precooked polenta is often not refrigerated and can be found in the pasta aisle at the supermarket.

Corned Beef and Cabbage with Country Mustard Sauce

What could be better on St. Patrick's Day than a casserole starring that trio of Irish favorites—corned beef, cabbage, and potatoes. Here they are bound with a delectable white sauce enriched generously with grated Gruyère, grainy mustard, and some crushed caraway seeds. This dish can be prepared several hours ahead, and then will need less than half an hour in the oven.

Serves 6

PREP TIME:
20 minutes

START-TO-FINISH TIME:
1 hour, 20 minutes

MAKE AHEAD:
Yes

Country Mustard Sauce

2 tbsp unsalted butter

2 tbsp all-purpose flour

2 cups/480 ml half-and-half

¼ cup/60 ml coarse-grain Dijon mustard

2 tsp caraway seeds, toasted and crushed (see page 12)

¼ tsp kosher salt

⅛ tsp cayenne pepper

Freshly ground black pepper

2½ cups/200 g grated Gruyère cheese

Corned Beef and Cabbage

1 medium head green cabbage

4 tbsp/55 g unsalted butter

12 oz/340 g small red-skin potatoes (1½ to 2 in/4 to 5 cm in diameter), scrubbed but not peeled

12 oz/340 g corned beef, thinly sliced and cut into strips 3 to 5 in/7.5 to 12 cm long and ½ in/6 mm wide (see Market Note)

Kosher salt

½ cup/40 g grated Gruyère cheese

2 tbsp chopped fresh dill

1. Arrange a rack in the middle of the oven and preheat to 375°F/190°C. Generously butter a 9-by-13-in/23-by-33-cm or another shallow 3-qt/2.8-L baking dish.

2. For the Country Mustard Sauce: Melt the butter in a medium saucepan over medium heat. Add the flour and cook, stirring constantly, for 1½ to 2 minutes. Gradually pour in the half-and-half and whisk constantly until the mixture is smooth and starts to simmer. Stir in the mustard, caraway seeds, salt, cayenne, and several grinds of black pepper, and then gradually whisk in the Gruyère. Remove from the heat and set aside.

3. For the Corned Beef and Cabbage: Quarter and core the cabbage. Cut the quarters crosswise into ½-in-/12-mm-wide strips to equal 10 cups/1.1 kg. (You may have some cabbage left over; save for another use.)

4. Melt the butter in a large, heavy frying pan over medium heat. When hot, add half of the cabbage and cook, stirring, until it starts to wilt; then add the remaining cabbage. Cook, stirring often, until the cabbage has softened and is starting to brown lightly, about 10 minutes. Remove to a large mixing bowl.

5. Bring a large saucepan of lightly salted water to a boil over high heat. Add the potatoes and cook until tender when pierced with a sharp knife, 12 to 15 minutes. Drain in a colander and, when cool enough to handle, cut into ¼-in-/ 6-mm-thick slices. Add to the mixing bowl holding the cabbage along with the corned beef strips. Add the sauce and toss to combine. Season with salt if needed.

6. Spread the cabbage mixture evenly in the baking dish. Sprinkle with the Gruyère. (The casserole can be prepared up to this point 4 hours ahead; cover and refrigerate. Bring to room temperature 30 minutes to 1 hour before baking.)

7. Bake, uncovered, until the casserole is hot and the cheese has melted, 20 to 25 minutes. Remove from the oven and cool for 15 minutes. Sprinkle with the dill before serving.

 MARKET NOTE:

Be sure to buy the best-quality corned beef available, preferably from a deli or the deli counter at the supermarket. Don't be afraid to ask the salesperson for a sample of different corned beef brands—you might be surprised by how much they vary in taste.

Baked Veal Shanks alla Primavera

This springtime osso buco is lightened by a bounty of seasonal produce. Veal shanks, cooked slowly in a simmering broth and wine until fork-tender, are then enhanced by a flavorful addition of spring onions, snow peas, and mushrooms. This casserole is an investment of your time, but you will be rewarded with an impressive all-in-one-dish meal.

Serves 6

PREP TIME:
25 minutes

START-TO-FINISH TIME:
2 hours, 20 minutes

MAKE AHEAD:
Yes

FREEZE:
Yes, after baking, but before adding the mushrooms, snow peas, and peas (see directions on page 11)

6 veal shanks, about 1 in/2.5 cm thick (about 3 lb/1.4 kg total)

Kosher salt

Freshly ground black pepper

¼ cup/30 g all-purpose flour

⅓ cup/75 ml olive oil, plus more as needed

1 cup/130 g spring onions (including 1 in/2.5 cm of the green stems), sliced ¼ in/6 mm thick (see Market Note)

1 cup/135 g diagonally sliced carrots (cut ¼ in/6 mm thick)

¾ cup/85 g diagonally sliced celery (cut ¼ in/6 mm thick)

3 cups/720 ml reduced-sodium chicken broth

1 cup/240 ml dry white wine

2 strips lemon zest about 3 in/7.5 cm long and 1 in/2.5 cm wide, plus 1 tbsp grated zest for garnish

3 medium garlic cloves, crushed and peeled

8 oz/225 g brown mushrooms (cremini), quartered through the stems

4 oz/115 g snow peas, ends trimmed, strings removed, halved crosswise on the diagonal

1 cup/145 g shelled fresh peas or frozen peas, defrosted

3 tbsp chopped fresh dill

1. Arrange a rack in the middle of the oven and preheat to 375°F/190°C.

2. Pat the veal shanks dry. Combine 1 tsp salt and ½ tsp pepper in a small bowl and season the veal on both sides. Spread the flour on a dinner plate and dredge the shanks in the flour, shaking off any excess. Reserve any remaining flour.

3. Heat the olive oil in an extra-large, ovenproof frying pan (with a lid) over medium-high heat. (If you don't have a large enough frying pan, use a large flameproof baking pan and, before baking, cover tightly with a double thickness of foil.) When the oil is hot, brown the veal well, about 4 minutes per side. Remove the veal to a platter.

4. If necessary, add enough oil to the frying pan in which the veal was sautéed to make 2 tbsp. When the oil is hot, add the spring onions, carrots, and celery, stirring until slightly softened, about 3 minutes. Sprinkle the reserved flour over the vegetables and cook, stirring, for 1½ to 2 minutes. Return the veal to the pan and add the chicken broth, wine, lemon zest strips, and garlic. Bring to a simmer and season the mixture with salt and pepper. Cover and transfer the frying pan to the oven.

5. Bake the veal for 45 minutes. Remove the lid and cook until the meat is very tender when pierced with a sharp knife and the liquids have reduced and thickened, about 45 minutes. (The veal can be prepared 2 days ahead; cool, cover, and refrigerate. Reheat in a preheated 375°F/190°C oven until hot, about 30 minutes, before continuing with the recipe.)

6. Remove the frying pan from the oven and stir in the mushrooms, snow peas, and peas. Return to the oven and cook, uncovered, until the vegetables are tender, about 8 minutes.

7. Combine the dill and grated lemon zest in a small bowl. Sprinkle the dill-lemon mixture over the veal and serve from the frying pan.

 MARKET NOTE:

Spring onions, as their name implies, are available in the spring. Like green onions, they have long green stems, but their white bulbs are larger, usually about 1 in/2.5 cm in diameter. They have a more defined taste than green onions and work well in this dish. If you can't find them, substitute chopped green onions, including 2 in/5 cm of the green stems, or chopped onion.

Veal Scallops on a Bed of Mushrooms

When my friend Brigitte Bizot, Parisian cook and host par excellence, brought a piping hot dish of veal scallops set atop an ethereally light mushroom flan to the table at a dinner party, I knew I wanted the recipe. The thinly sliced meat had been sautéed until golden brown, arranged over a savory mélange of mushrooms and shallots, and then topped with a creamy sauce. Here was a casserole that was both sophisticated and homey at the same time. The talented cook willingly shared the recipe, pointing out that the mushrooms could be baked ahead. At serving time, she explained, all that is necessary is to quickly sauté the veal and turn the pan juices into a sauce.

Serves 4 to 6

PREP TIME:
30 minutes

START-TO-FINISH TIME:
1 hour, 45 minutes

MAKE AHEAD:
Yes, partially

Mushroom Flan

3 tbsp unsalted butter

3 tbsp vegetable oil

1½ lb/680 g white mushrooms, cleaned and
　　cut into ¼-in-/6-mm-thick slices

6 tbsp/40 g chopped shallots

1½ tbsp all-purpose flour

1½ cups/360 ml whole milk

¼ cup/60 ml crème fraîche, homemade (see
　　page 12) or store-bought

¼ cup/30 g grated Parmesan cheese,
　　preferably Parmigiano-Reggiano

1½ tbsp chopped fresh flat-leaf parsley

Kosher salt

Freshly ground black pepper

3 egg yolks

8 veal scallops (about 3 oz/85 g each), about
　　¼ in/6 mm thick (see Cooking Tip)

Kosher salt

Freshly ground black pepper

1. Arrange a rack in the middle of the oven and preheat to 350°F/180°C. Generously butter a 9-by-13-in/23-by-33-cm or another shallow 3-qt/2.8-L baking dish.

2. For the Mushroom Flan: Melt the butter with the vegetable oil in a large, heavy frying pan over medium-high heat. When very hot, add the mushrooms and cook, stirring occasionally, until browned and all the liquid has evaporated, about 10 minutes. Add the shallots and cook, stirring, until softened, 2 to 3 minutes.

3. Sprinkle the mushrooms and shallots with the flour and cook, stirring, for 1 minute. Add the milk and bring to a gentle boil, stirring constantly until the mixture thickens enough to coat the back of a spoon, 3 to 4 minutes. Turn the heat off and cool the mushroom mixture in the pan for 10 minutes. Transfer to a food processor and pulse several times until the mushrooms are coarsely chopped.

4. Transfer the mushroom mixture to a large bowl and add the crème fraîche, Parmesan, and parsley. Mix well and season with ½ tsp salt and ⅛ tsp pepper. Season with more salt if needed. Add the egg yolks and mix well. Spread the mushroom mixture evenly in the prepared baking dish and bake,

uncovered, until set, 30 to 35 minutes. Remove from the oven and cover loosely with foil. (The flan can be prepared 6 hours ahead; cool, cover, and refrigerate. Reheat in a 350°F/180°C oven until heated through, 15 to 20 minutes.)

5. While the flan is in the oven, pat the veal dry with paper towels and season generously on both sides with salt and pepper. In a large, heavy frying pan over medium-high heat, heat the butter and olive oil until very hot. Add as many veal scallops as will fit comfortably in a single layer and sauté until browned, 3 minutes per side. Remove to a plate and repeat with the remaining veal. Cover loosely with foil and set aside.

6. Add the wine to the frying pan and deglaze the pan with a whisk, scraping any browned bits on the bottom into the liquid. Whisk in the cream, crème fraîche, and Parmesan. Cook for 1 to 2 minutes or until the sauce thickens. Taste and season the sauce with salt if needed.

7. Arrange the veal scallops, slightly overlapping, on top of the mushroom flan, and ladle the sauce over them. Sprinkle the veal with the almonds and parsley before serving.

1½ tbsp unsalted butter

1½ tbsp olive oil

½ cup/120 ml dry white wine

½ cup/120 ml heavy or whipping cream

¼ cup/60 ml crème fraîche, homemade (see page 12) or store-bought

¼ cup/30 g grated Parmesan cheese, preferably Parmigiano-Reggiano

3 tbsp sliced almonds, toasted (see page 12)

1½ tbsp chopped fresh flat-leaf parsley

COOKING TIP:

If your veal is thicker than ¼ in/6 mm, place each scallop between two sheets of waxed paper and pound to the right thickness.

Thin chicken cutlets (¼ in/6 mm thick) can be substituted for the veal, with great results.

Cold Nights Sausage and Potato Gratin

If you love German potato salad, you'll enjoy this dish of sliced red-skin potatoes and kielbasa sausage, coated with a warm bacon-scented dressing. Mustard adds a piquant note, while fresh dill provides refreshing accents of color and flavor. Serve this casserole with a salad of frisée, thinly sliced apples, and walnuts in a vinaigrette.

Serves 6

PREP TIME:
20 minutes

START-TO-FINISH TIME:
1 hour, 20 minutes

MAKE AHEAD:
Yes

1½ lb/680 g small red-skin potatoes (1½ to 2 in/4 to 5 cm in diameter), scrubbed but not peeled

Kosher salt

4 strips smoked bacon

Butter for sautéing, if necessary

12 oz/340 g kielbasa, sliced into ¼-in-/6-mm-thick rounds (see Cooking Tip)

1½ cups/190 g chopped onion

1 cup/240 ml cider vinegar

1 cup/240 ml water

1 tbsp plus 1 tsp sugar

1 tbsp plus 1 tsp coarse-grain Dijon mustard

Freshly ground black pepper

2 to 3 tsp Wondra flour (see Cooking Tip)

¼ cup plus 2 tbsp/15 g chopped fresh dill

1 cup/240 ml sour cream

½ cup/30 g Toasted Bread Crumbs (page 12), made with butter

1. Arrange a rack in the middle of the oven and preheat to 350°F/180°C. Generously butter a 9-by-13-in/23-by-33-cm or another shallow 3-qt/2.8-L baking dish.

2. Bring a large pot of water to a boil over high heat and add the potatoes and 1 tbsp salt. Return to a boil and cook the potatoes until tender when pierced with a knife, 12 to 15 minutes. (Don't overcook or the potatoes will be mushy.) Drain in a colander and cool slightly until you can handle them comfortably. Cut into ¼-in-/6-mm-thick slices and put them in the prepared baking dish.

3. In a large, heavy frying pan over medium heat, sauté the bacon until browned and crisp, about 4 minutes. Remove with a slotted spoon and drain on paper towels. Pour off all but 3 tbsp of the drippings in the pan and return to medium heat. If necessary, melt extra butter to make this amount. Add the kielbasa to the pan and sauté, stirring, until just starting to brown, 3 to 4 minutes. Remove the kielbasa to the baking dish.

4. Add the onion to the same frying pan and sauté, stirring, until softened and lightly browned, 3 to 4 minutes. Whisk in the vinegar, water, sugar, mustard, ½ tsp salt, and ½ tsp pepper. Bring to a simmer and continue simmering until the liquid has reduced by about one-third, 2 to 3 minutes. Sprinkle the Wondra flour over the mixture and cook, whisking constantly, until it has dissolved and the onion mixture has thickened slightly, about 2 minutes.

5. Pour the onion mixture over the potatoes and kielbasa in the baking dish and toss gently to coat. Season generously with salt and pepper and stir in ¼ cup/10 g of the dill. Using a spatula or table knife, spread the sour cream in a very thin layer over the sausage and potatoes. (The casserole can be prepared up to this point 4 hours ahead; cover and refrigerate. Bring to room temperature 30 minutes to 1 hour before baking.) Crumble the bacon and sprinkle it over the casserole, followed by the bread crumbs.

6. Bake, uncovered, until the potatoes are tender when pierced with a sharp knife, about 20 minutes. Remove from the oven and sprinkle with the remaining 2 tbsp dill before serving.

COOKING TIP:

Lighter turkey kielbasa can be substituted for regular kielbasa in this dish with excellent results.

Wondra (a brand name) flour is very finely ground flour that dissolves almost instantly in liquids. It is sold in most supermarkets. If unavailable, put the same amount of all-purpose flour in a bowl, add an equal amount of water, and stir to make a smooth paste.

Cassoulet Rapide

When my friend Jacques Ableman told me that he routinely makes a quick version of cassoulet—that famous French casserole of beans, sausages, meats, and poultry that takes days or a marathon cooking session to assemble—I was curious and asked for his recipe. He explained that he buys good smoked sausages and slab bacon and quickly panfries them, along with pieces of *confit de canard* (cooked duck). He uses canned beans, enhancing them with sautéed vegetables and crushed rosemary and fennel seeds. He then cooks this robust mixture in white wine. I adapted his version by replacing the duck with meaty chicken thighs, and including broth as well as wine. *Et voilà*—a mouthwatering cassoulet that takes less than two hours to prep and bake!

Serves 6

PREP TIME:
30 minutes

START-TO-FINISH TIME:
1 hour, 45 minutes

MAKE AHEAD:
Yes

FREEZE:
Yes, after baking (see directions on page 11)

4 oz/115 g slab or thickly sliced smoked bacon

1 tbsp olive oil

12 oz/340 g smoked kielbasa, halved lengthwise and cut diagonally into 2-in/5-cm lengths

6 chicken thighs (1¾ lb/800 g total)

Kosher salt

Freshly ground black pepper

2 cups/255 g halved and thinly sliced onions

1 cup/135 g thinly sliced carrots

5 medium garlic cloves, peeled and smashed

Four 15-oz/430-g cans cannellini beans, rinsed and drained well

One 15-oz/430-g can diced tomatoes, drained

2 tbsp tomato paste

1 tbsp crushed dried rosemary (see Market Note on page 34), plus fresh rosemary sprigs for garnish (optional)

1½ tsp fennel seeds, crushed (see page 12)

2 cups/480 ml reduced-sodium chicken broth

1 cup/240 ml dry white wine

6 slices good-quality artisan-style country bread, sliced ½ in/12 mm thick and lightly toasted

1. Arrange a rack in the middle of the oven and preheat to 400°F/200°C. Have ready a 9-by-13-in/23-by-33-cm or another shallow 3-qt/2.8-L baking dish.

2. If using slab bacon, cut into strips ¼ in/6 mm thick, 1½ in/4 cm long, and ½ in/12 mm wide. Or cut thickly sliced bacon crosswise into 1 in/2.5 cm pieces.

3. Heat the olive oil in a large, heavy frying pan over medium heat. When hot, add the kielbasa and cook, stirring often, until lightly browned, 4 to 5 minutes. Remove and drain on paper towels. Leave the drippings in the pan and add the bacon; sauté until slightly crisp and golden brown, 4 to 5 minutes. Remove and drain on paper towels.

4. Remove the pan from the heat and pour off all but 3 tbsp of the drippings. Pat the chicken dry with paper towels and season generously on both sides with salt and pepper. Return the pan to medium heat, and add enough thighs to fit in a single layer. Sauté until well browned, 4 to 5 minutes per side. Remove and set aside. Repeat with the remaining chicken.

continued . . .

5. Pour off all but 2 tbsp of the drippings in the pan, and place over medium heat. Add the onions, carrots, and garlic and cook, stirring often, until softened, about 5 minutes.

6. Add the beans, tomatoes, tomato paste, crushed rosemary, and fennel seeds. Season the mixture with 1¼ tsp salt and ¾ tsp pepper, and then stir in the chicken broth and wine. Bring to a simmer. Cook, stirring occasionally, for 5 minutes.

7. Scatter the kielbasa and bacon evenly in the bottom of the baking dish, and then nestle the chicken thighs in the dish. Ladle the bean mixture and juices over the meats. Bake, uncovered, until the chicken thighs are tender when pricked with a sharp knife and most (but not all) of the liquids have evaporated, about 40 minutes. (The casserole can be prepared 2 days ahead; cool, cover, and refrigerate. Reheat in a preheated 350°F/180°C oven until hot, 30 to 40 minutes.)

8. Remove the cassoulet from the oven and serve with the slices of toasted bread. If you like, garnish the center of the dish with a few fresh rosemary sprigs.

Cider-Baked Pork, Red Cabbage, and Apples

When the first fresh cider arrives in the market each fall, I buy it for sipping, but also for cooking hearty dishes like this casserole. Red cabbage, onions, and apples are sautéed in butter, simmered in cider, and then spread in a baking dish to make a bed for panfried slices of pork tenderloin. After the casserole has been baked, the pork is fork-tender and so are the deep burgundy–hued cabbage and apples.

Serves 6

PREP TIME:
30 minutes

START-TO-FINISH TIME:
1 hour, 50 minutes

MAKE AHEAD:
Yes

1 small head red cabbage

3 tart and firm apples (Granny Smith, Jonathan, or Macoun work well)

5 tbsp/70 g unsalted butter

1½ cups/190 g thinly sliced onions

1½ tbsp sugar

4½ tbsp/70 ml cider vinegar

1 tbsp fennel seeds, crushed (see page 12)

Kosher salt

3 cups/720 ml cider

2 pork tenderloins (about 1 lb/455 g each), trimmed of silver skin and excess fat

½ tsp freshly ground black pepper

3 tbsp canola oil

1 tbsp chopped fresh flat-leaf parsley

1. Arrange a rack in the middle of the oven and preheat to 375°F/190°C. Generously butter a 9-by-13-in/23-by-33-cm or another shallow 3-qt/2.8-L baking dish.

2. Quarter and core the cabbage. Cut each quarter crosswise into ¼-in-/6-mm-wide strips to get 6 cups/655 g. (Save any leftover cabbage for another use.) Quarter and core the unpeeled apples, and then cut the quarters lengthwise into ¼-in-/6-mm-thick slices.

3. Melt 3 tbsp of the butter in a large, heavy frying pan over medium heat. When hot, add the cabbage and onions. Sauté the mixture, stirring, until just starting to soften, about 5 minutes. Stir in the apples, sugar, vinegar, fennel seeds, and 2½ tsp salt and cook, stirring, for 5 minutes. Pour in 2 cups/480 ml of the cider and bring the mixture to a simmer. Reduce the heat to low, cover, and continue simmering until the cabbage and apples are tender, about 20 minutes. Taste the cabbage and season with more salt if needed. Transfer the cabbage mixture, along with any juices, to the prepared baking dish.

4. Cut each pork tenderloin into 1-in-/2.5-cm-thick slices. In a small bowl, mix together 1 tsp salt and the pepper. Season the pork slices on both sides with this mixture.

continued . . .

5. Heat the canola oil in a large, heavy frying pan over medium-high heat until very hot, but not smoking, Add half of the pork slices and brown lightly, 1 minute or more per side. Remove to a dinner plate and repeat with the remaining pork. Add the remaining 1 cup/240 ml cider to the frying pan and cook until reduced by half, whisking the browned bits on the bottom of the pan into the cider, 2 to 3 minutes or more. Whisk in the remaining 2 tbsp butter and any juices that have collected on the plate with the pork.

6. Arrange the pork slices on top of the cabbage mixture. Spoon the reduced cider over the slices. (The casserole can be prepared up to this point 4 hours ahead; cover and refrigerate. Bring to room temperature 1 hour before continuing with the recipe.)

7. Bake the casserole, uncovered, until an instant-read thermometer registers 145°F/63°C when inserted into the center of a pork slice, about 25 minutes. Remove from the oven and let the casserole stand for 10 minutes.

8. Garnish the pork with a sprinkling of parsley before serving.

Saffron Rice Pilaf with Lamb Meatballs, Red Peppers, and Dates

Easy, delicious, and different is how I would describe this casserole. Petite meatballs prepared with ground lamb and seasoned with Moroccan spices are nestled into a baked rice pilaf during the last few minutes of cooking. The rice, scented with saffron, cooks to a rich, golden yellow and is accented with bits of red bell pepper and Medjool dates.

Serves 4 to 6

PREP TIME:
20 minutes

START-TO-FINISH TIME:
1 hour

MAKE AHEAD:
Yes, partially

Lamb Meatballs

1 tbsp ground cumin

2 tsp paprika

1 tsp kosher salt

¼ tsp cayenne pepper

1 lb/455 g ground lamb

¼ cup/30 g very finely chopped onion

2 tsp minced garlic

2 tbsp olive oil

1¼ cups/270 g long-grain rice, preferably basmati

¾ cup/115 g red bell pepper cut into strips, ¼ in/6 mm wide and 1½ in/4 cm long

8 Medjool dates, pitted and cut lengthwise into quarters

3½ cups/840 ml reduced-sodium chicken broth

¼ tsp saffron threads, crushed

Kosher salt

3 tbsp julienned fresh flat-leaf parsley

3 tbsp julienned fresh mint

2 tsp julienned lemon zest

1. Arrange a rack in the middle of the oven and preheat to 375°F/190°C. Oil a shallow 2½-qt/2.4-L baking dish.

2. For the Lamb Meatballs: In a medium bowl, mix together the cumin, paprika, salt, and cayenne. Add the lamb, onion, and garlic and mix with two forks to combine well. Scoop 1 tbsp of the lamb mixture into your hands and roll into a small ball. Repeat until all the mixture has been used. You should get about twenty-four meatballs. (The meatballs can be prepared to this point 1 day ahead; cover and refrigerate. Bring to room temperature at least 30 minutes or up to 1 hour before continuing with the recipe.)

3. Heat the olive oil in a heavy, large frying pan over medium-high heat. When hot, add the meatballs and brown on all sides, 2 to 3 minutes. Set aside.

4. Spread the rice evenly in the prepared baking dish, and then scatter the bell pepper and dates over the rice.

5. Heat the chicken broth in a medium saucepan, covered, over medium heat until it simmers. Add the saffron, taste the broth, and season with salt if needed. Pour the hot broth over the rice. Cover the dish tightly with foil and bake until almost all the liquid has been absorbed and the rice is tender, about 20 minutes. Remove the casserole from the oven and carefully remove the foil. Stir in the meatballs, re-cover, and bake 5 minutes more. Remove from the oven.

6. Combine the parsley, mint, and lemon zest in a small bowl and sprinkle over the casserole before serving.

SEAFOOD SPECIALS

Shellfish and Fish, All in One Dish

You don't need to reach for a tin of tuna or salmon when your heart is set on an all-in-one seafood dish. Fresh fish, rather than canned, is the focus of this chapter. Shellfish, including shrimp, sea scallops, lobster, and even oysters, star in the following recipes, together with popular choices such as cod, salmon, and halibut.

When including fresh fish in casseroles, it is essential to pay attention to both the temperature of the oven and the cooking time. If the oven is too hot or the dish is cooked too long, the fish can dry out. To ease this concern, I have carefully timed these recipes, sometimes adding fish at the halfway point or even at the end of the baking, to ensure that it remains moist. For example, in luscious New England Lobster and Corn Casserole (page 73), the lobster goes in after the casserole has been in the oven for a while, and for Shrimp Baked in Coconut and Lime Rice (page 64), the shellfish are stirred in during the last few minutes of cooking.

Seafood pairs well with rice and potatoes, and you'll discover some especially enticing combinations here. The Sea Scallops Nestled in Piperade (page 69), which are baked on a bed of saffron-scented rice, are vibrantly flavored. One of my favorite recipes is a "Fish and Chips" Casserole (page 74), in which pieces of cod are covered with creamy scalloped potatoes and baked until the fish is tender and flaky and the spuds topping is golden and crisp.

Lighter and often more healthful than the canned-fish creations of yesteryear, these dishes are not complicated, and they take only an hour or so from start to finish to prepare. Save that can of tuna for sandwiches, and bring these updated seafood casseroles to your table instead.

Shrimp Baked in Coconut and Lime Rice

For this delectable dish with Southeast Asian accents, jasmine rice is cooked in coconut milk, which provides a hint of sweetness to the casserole. Lime juice and zest counter with a citrus note, while fish sauce provides a salty tang, and serrano pepper and ginger offer a bit of heat. The rice is baked until almost done, and then shrimp and fresh mango are stirred in for a few extra minutes of cooking.

Serves 6

PREP TIME:
30 minutes

START-TO-FINISH TIME:
1 hour, 20 minutes

MAKE AHEAD:
No

One 13½-oz/405-ml can coconut milk (see Market Note)

1½ cups/360 ml reduced-sodium chicken broth

2 tbsp fresh lime juice, plus 2 tsp grated lime zest

2 tbsp sliced lemongrass (about 2 stalks; see Market Note)

1 tbsp fish sauce

1 tbsp seeded and finely chopped serrano pepper

Kosher salt

1½ cups/320 g jasmine or another long-grain rice (see Market Note)

1 lb/455 g large shrimp (16 to 20 count), peeled and deveined

1 ripe mango, pitted, peeled, and cut into ¼-in/6-mm dice

2 tsp finely chopped fresh ginger

½ cup/55 g salted roasted peanuts, coarsely chopped

¼ cup/10 g chopped fresh cilantro

1. Arrange a rack in the middle of the oven and preheat to 350°F/180°C. Oil a shallow 3-qt/2.8-L baking dish.

2. Stir the coconut milk well to blend and pour it into a large, heavy saucepan. Add the chicken broth, lime juice, lemongrass, and fish sauce and whisk well to combine. Place the pan over medium heat and simmer for 2 minutes. Strain the liquid into a bowl and stir in the serrano pepper and 1 tsp of the lime zest. Taste a spoonful of the liquid and season with salt if needed.

3. Spread the rice in the prepared baking dish, pour the hot liquid over it, and mix well to combine. Cover the dish tightly with foil and bake until the rice is tender and has absorbed most of the liquid, 25 to 30 minutes.

4. While the rice is cooking, pat the shrimp dry and salt them. Toss the shrimp, diced mango, and ginger together in a medium bowl.

5. When the rice is almost cooked, remove the dish from the oven and carefully remove the foil. Stir in the shrimp and mango mixture. Replace the foil, covering the dish tightly, and return to the oven. Bake until the shrimp are pink and cooked through, 8 to 10 minutes.

6. Remove the casserole from the oven. Combine the peanuts, cilantro, and the remaining 1 tsp lime zest in a small bowl and mix well. Sprinkle over the casserole before serving.

 MARKET NOTE:

Coconut milk can be found in most groceries, often in the section where foreign ingredients are displayed. Both light and regular coconut milk are available, and either will work in this dish.

Lemongrass—long, slightly woody, grayish-green stalks about the size of green onions—can be found in the produce section of many groceries and in Asian markets. It has a slightly sour, lemony taste and is an important ingredient in Thai and Vietnamese cooking. Store it in a plastic bag for up to 2 weeks in the refrigerator. To chop lemongrass, first remove the tough outer layers and trim about 1 in/2.5 cm off the woody base from each stalk. Then, starting at the base, slice each stalk thinly, stopping where the leaves begin to branch off.

Jasmine rice, a fragrant, long-grain rice used in Asian cooking, is available in many groceries. If you cannot find it, basmati rice can be used.

New Orleans Shrimp and Andouille Jambalaya

During my childhood, I spent many summer vacations at my grandmother's home, in a small Mississippi town just north of New Orleans. A gifted Southern cook, she used the luscious shrimp from the nearby Gulf Coast to make countless dishes, including classic jambalaya. In her version, the rice was cooked separately and then topped with a spicy tomato-based sauce, but in this recipe, the two are conveniently baked together in a casserole. Large shrimp are added to the spicy mélange during the last few minutes in the oven.

Serves 6

PREP TIME:
30 minutes

START-TO-FINISH TIME:
1 hour, 30 minutes

MAKE AHEAD:
No

12 oz/340 g andouille sausages

2 tbsp olive oil

1½ cups/190 g chopped onion

1 cup/115 g chopped celery

1 cup/130 g diced red bell pepper

1 tbsp chopped garlic

Two 15-oz/430-g cans diced tomatoes, with their juices

5 cups/1.2 L reduced-sodium chicken broth

2 tbsp Worcestershire sauce

1 tbsp dried thyme

Kosher salt

⅛ tsp cayenne pepper

2 bay leaves, broken in half

2 cups/430 g long-grain rice, preferably basmati

18 large (16 to 20 count) shrimp (about 1 lb/455 g), preferably Gulf Coast, peeled and deveined

½ cup/60 g chopped green onions (including 2 in/5 cm of the green stems)

1. Arrange a rack in the middle of the oven and preheat to 350°F/180°C. Generously oil a 9-by-13-in/23-by-33-cm or another shallow 3-qt/2.8-L baking dish.

2. Halve the andouille sausages lengthwise, and then cut crosswise into ⅛-in-/3-mm-thick slices. Heat the olive oil in a large, heavy frying pan over medium heat. When hot, add the sausages, and cook, stirring, until lightly browned, 3 to 4 minutes. Remove with a slotted spoon and drain on paper towels.

3. Pour off all but 1 tbsp of the drippings in the frying pan and set over medium heat. Add the onion, celery, and bell pepper and cook, stirring, until the vegetables are just softened, about 4 minutes. Add the garlic and sauté for 1 minute more.

4. Stir in the tomatoes and their juices, the chicken broth, Worcestershire sauce, thyme, 1 tsp salt, the cayenne, and bay leaves. Bring the mixture to a simmer, and add the sausages. Taste and season with more salt if needed.

5. Spread the rice in the prepared baking dish. Set aside
    ½ cup/120 ml of the simmering tomato mixture in the fry-
    ing pan, and pour the remainder over the rice. Mix well to
    combine. Cover the dish tightly with foil. Bake until the rice
    is tender and has absorbed almost all of the liquid, about
    30 minutes.

6. Remove the dish from the oven and carefully remove the
    foil. Using a fork or spoon, arrange the shrimp on top of
    the casserole, pushing them slightly into the rice mixture.
    Ladle the reserved ½ cup/120 ml tomato mixture over
    the shrimp. Replace the foil, covering the dish tightly, and
    return to the oven. Bake until the shrimp are pink and
    cooked through, 8 to 10 minutes more.

7. Remove the bay leaves and sprinkle the dish with the green
    onions before serving.

Sea Scallops Nestled in Piperade

Large sea scallops seasoned with a robust mixture of smoked paprika and cumin are delicious when baked on a bed of piperade and saffron rice. A Basque dish, piperade is a brightly hued mixture of sautéed bell peppers, tomatoes, and onions, scented with *piment d'Espelette* (a spicy red pepper powder). A little cayenne pepper stands in for the Espelette powder in these individual layered casseroles.

Serves 4

PREP TIME:
30 min

START-TO-FINISH TIME:
1 hour, 30 minutes

MAKE AHEAD:
Yes, partially

Piperade

3 tbsp olive oil

1 cup/125 g chopped onion

⅔ cup/100 g chopped red bell pepper
(¼-in/6-mm pieces)

⅔ cup/100 g chopped yellow bell pepper
(¼-in/6-mm pieces)

1 tbsp minced garlic

Kosher salt

Pinch of cayenne pepper

1 cup/185 g grape tomatoes, quartered
lengthwise, but not seeded

2 to 3 tsp sherry wine vinegar

Saffron Rice

1 tbsp unsalted butter

1 cup/215 g long-grain rice, preferably basmati

2 cups/280 ml water

⅛ tsp saffron threads, crushed

½ tsp kosher salt

1. Arrange a rack in the middle of the oven and preheat to 400°F/200°C. Lightly oil four 6- to 7-in/15- to 17-cm gratin dishes or 1-cup/240-ml ramekins.

2. For the Piperade: Heat the olive oil in a large, heavy frying pan over medium heat. When the oil is hot, add the onion and red and yellow bell peppers. Cook, stirring, until softened, 4 to 5 minutes. Add the garlic, ½ tsp salt, and the cayenne; cook, stirring, for 1 minute more. Remove from the heat and stir in the tomatoes. Gradually stir in 2 tsp sherry vinegar; taste and add more vinegar and salt if desired. (The piperade can be prepared 1 day ahead; cool, cover, and refrigerate. Reheat over medium heat until hot, 3 to 4 minutes.)

3. For the Saffron Rice: Melt the butter in a medium, heavy saucepan (with a lid) over medium heat. When hot, add the rice and stir for a few seconds, until all the grains are lightly coated in butter. Add the water, crushed saffron, and salt. Stir well and bring to a simmer. Reduce the heat to low, cover the rice, and cook until all the liquid has been absorbed, 15 to 20 minutes. Remove from the heat. (The rice can stand, covered, for 30 minutes.)

continued . . .

4. For the scallops: In a small saucepan over low heat, melt the butter. Add the smoked paprika, cumin, and salt and remove from the heat. Pat the scallops dry with paper towels, and then gently toss a few at a time in the smoked paprika mixture.

5. Divide the rice among the prepared dishes and spread it on the bottom of each one. Spread a quarter of the piperade on top of each dish of rice. Nestle 3 scallops into each dish. Place the dishes on a baking sheet. Bake until the scallops are cooked through, 12 to 14 minutes. To check for doneness, gently pierce a few scallops with a small knife to see if they are opaque.

6. Remove the dishes from the oven, sprinkle the scallops with chopped parsley, and serve immediately.

Scallops

1½ tbsp unsalted butter

1 tsp Spanish smoked paprika
 (see Market Note)

⅜ tsp ground cumin

⅜ tsp kosher salt

12 large sea scallops (about 1 to 1¼ lb/
 455 to 570 g), side muscles removed

2 tbsp chopped fresh flat-leaf parsley

 MARKET NOTE:

Spanish smoked paprika, called *pimentón*, is available in gourmet food stores, in some groceries, and online from Penzeys at www .penzeys.com. *Pimentón* comes sweet *(dulce)*, medium-hot *(agridulce)*, and hot *(picante)*. For this recipe, use the sweet.

Aunt Janie's Lemon-Parsley Oysters with Cracker Topping

My Aunt Janie, a gifted cook from Mississippi, gave me the recipe for Johnny Reb baked oysters many years ago. (Johnny Rebel was the moniker the Union army used for Confederate soldiers.) She swore that this was her favorite way to prepare these bivalves. Nothing could be simpler. Freshly shucked oysters, sprinkled with parsley and shallots, are layered in a baking dish, and then drizzled with lemon juice and half-and-half. Black pepper and hot sauce add a touch of heat to this casserole, while a crushed cracker crust provides some crunch. When baked, the cracker topping is golden and crisp and the oysters, velvety-tender beneath.

Serves 3 to 4

PREP TIME:
45 minutes

START-TO-FINISH TIME:
1 hour, 10 minutes

MAKE AHEAD:
No

1 qt/455 g fresh-shucked oysters, drained

¼ cup/10 g finely chopped fresh flat-leaf parsley

¼ cup/40 g finely chopped shallots

½ tsp kosher salt

½ tsp freshly ground black pepper

About 4 quick splashes hot pepper sauce, preferably Tabasco sauce

1½ tsp Worcestershire sauce

1 tbsp fresh lemon juice

6 tbsp/90 ml half-and-half

4 tbsp/55 g unsalted butter, melted

1 cup/100 g fine cracker crumbs made from oyster cracker or saltines

Paprika, preferably Hungarian, for sprinkling

1. Arrange a rack in the middle of the oven and preheat to 375°F/190°C. Generously butter a shallow 1½- to 2-qt/ 1.4- to 2-L baking dish.

2. Place half of the oysters in the prepared baking dish. Sprinkle them with half each of the parsley, shallots, salt, pepper, hot pepper sauce, Worcestershire sauce, lemon juice, and half-and-half. Combine the melted butter and cracker crumbs, and scatter half of this mixture on top. Repeat to make a second layer of oysters, seasonings, and butter and cracker crumbs. Sprinkle generously with paprika.

3. Bake, uncovered, for 20 minutes; the top should be golden and crisp. If not, arrange a rack 4 to 5 in/10 to 12 cm from the broiler and broil the casserole for 2 to 3 minutes, watching constantly to avoid burning. Serve warm.

COOKING TIP:

This recipe can be doubled easily; use a 2- to 2½-qt/2- to 2.4-L baking dish and bake for 8 to 10 minutes longer.

New England Lobster and Corn Casserole

Three summer staples of New England cooking—lobster, corn, and potatoes—make an appearance in this dish. The secret to this casserole's success lies in baking the corn and potato custard for several minutes, and then adding the cooked lobster. That way the coral-hued shellfish morsels don't dry out. This recipe serves four generously, but when the price of lobsters drops, I am always tempted to double the recipe!

Serves 4

PREP TIME:
20 minutes

START-TO-FINISH TIME:
1 hour, 30 minutes

MAKE AHEAD:
Yes, partially

1½ tbsp unsalted butter

1½ tbsp vegetable oil, plus ¼ cup/60 ml

2 cups/300 g fresh corn kernels (3 to 4 ears of corn)

⅔ lb/310 g red-skin potatoes, scrubbed, but not peeled, and cut into ¼- to ½-in/6- to 12-mm dice

1 cup/125 g chopped onion

¾ tsp kosher salt

Scant ⅛ tsp cayenne pepper

4 large eggs

1 cup/240 ml half-and-half

1 cup/240 ml crème fraîche, homemade (see page 12) or store-bought

1 cup/115 g grated Parmesan cheese, preferably Parmigiano-Reggiano

10 oz/280 g cooked lobster meat, cartilage removed, and cut into generous 1- to 1½-in/ 2.5- to 4-cm pieces (see Market Note)

¼ cup/10 g finely julienned fresh basil

🔲 MARKET NOTE:

Fresh-cooked lobster meat is available in many good fish markets. You can also cook the lobsters yourself. One pound/455 g of uncooked, live lobster yields about 4 oz/115 g of cooked meat.

1. Arrange a rack in the middle of the oven and preheat to 375°F/190°C. Generously butter a shallow 2-qt/2-L baking dish.

2. Heat the butter and 1½ tbsp vegetable oil in a large, heavy frying pan over medium heat until hot. Add the corn and sauté, stirring, until light golden, 5 to 6 minutes. Remove the corn from the pan and set aside.

3. Return the pan to medium heat and add the remaining ¼ cup/60 ml oil. When the oil is hot, add the diced potatoes and onion. Sauté, stirring constantly, until the vegetables are lightly browned and the potatoes are tender when pierced with a knife, 7 to 8 minutes. Remove the pan from the heat and stir in the corn, salt, and cayenne; set aside to cool for 5 minutes.

4. In a large bowl, whisk together the eggs, half-and-half, and crème fraîche. Stir in the Parmesan cheese, and then the corn and potato mixture. Transfer to the prepared baking dish. (The casserole can be made up to this point 30 minutes ahead; cover and leave at cool room temperature.)

5. Bake the casserole, uncovered, for 15 minutes, and then stir in the lobster, distributing it evenly. Bake until a knife inserted into the middle of the casserole comes out clean and the custard is set, 15 minutes or slightly more. Remove from the oven and cool for 5 minutes. Garnish the casserole with a sprinkling of basil before serving.

"Fish and Chips" Casserole

The fish is baked and the potatoes are scalloped in this interpretation of the famous duo. A luscious white sauce prepared with crème fraîche and infused with fresh thyme blankets the sliced Yukon golds, which in turn cover the chunks of cod. When done, the potato topping is golden and the fish beneath flaky and tender.

Serves 4

PREP TIME:
10 minutes

START-TO-FINISH TIME:
1 hour, 25 minutes

MAKE AHEAD:
No

1½ tbsp unsalted butter

1½ tbsp all-purpose flour

¾ cup/180 ml whole milk

¾ cup/180 ml crème fraîche, homemade
  (see page 12) or store-bought

1½ tsp minced garlic

Kosher salt

Freshly ground black pepper

2 fresh thyme sprigs, plus 1 tbsp chopped
  fresh thyme for garnish

1 to 1¼ lb/455 to 570 g thick (about ¾ in/2 cm)
  cod or haddock fillets (see Market Note)

1 lb/455g Yukon gold potatoes, preferably
  small to medium

1. Arrange a rack in the middle of the oven and preheat to 400°F/200°C. Generously butter a 2-qt/2-L shallow baking dish.

2. Melt the butter until hot in a medium saucepan over medium heat. Add the flour and cook, stirring constantly, for 1½ to 2 minutes. Gradually pour in the milk and crème fraîche, whisking constantly until the mixture comes to a simmer. Remove from the heat and stir in the garlic, ⅜ tsp salt, and ⅜ tsp black pepper. Add the thyme sprigs and let the sauce infuse with these seasonings for at least 10 minutes.

3. Cut the cod fillets into 1-in/2.5-cm chunks, and pat them dry with paper towels. Place the fish in the prepared baking dish and season generously with salt and several grinds of pepper. Remove the thyme sprigs from the sauce, and pour half of the sauce over the fish. Stir gently so that all the fish pieces are well coated, and spread them evenly in a single layer.

4. Peel the potatoes and cut them crosswise into very thin slices (⅛ in/3 mm thick or less). Arrange the potato slices in a single overlapping layer on top of the fish. (You may have a few slices leftover; save for another use or discard.) Season the potatoes with salt and several grinds of pepper. Pour the remaining sauce over the potatoes and spread evenly. (The casserole can be prepared up to this point 4 hours ahead; cover and refrigerate. Bring to room temperature 30 minutes before baking.)

5. Bake the casserole, uncovered, for 45 to 50 minutes. After 30 minutes, the potatoes will have just started to take on color and the liquids in the pan will be bubbling up slightly. At this point, start checking often until the potatoes are tender when pierced with a sharp knife and are golden.

6. Arrange a rack 4 to 5 in/10 to 12 cm from the broiler and broil the casserole until the potatoes are more browned, 1 to 2 minutes. Watch carefully as the potatoes can burn quickly.

7. Remove the casserole from the oven. Let stand for 5 to 10 minutes, and then sprinkle with thyme before serving.

 MARKET NOTE:

Ask the fishmonger for thick cod fillets, sometimes called cod loins. These will be easier to cut into 1-in/2.5-cm cubes and will hold up better while baking.

Baked Fish on a Bed of Spinach, Chickpeas, and Tomatoes

My son, who does all the cooking in his family, sent me this recipe, saying that it has become his salvation on hectic weeknights. He explained that it is an all-in-one-dish main course, which features fish fillets arranged on a bed of spinach, tomatoes, chickpeas, and olives, all conveniently layered in a casserole. The fish, scented with lemon and topped with homemade bread crumbs, emerges moist and the vegetables meld into a tender mélange.

Serves 4

PREP TIME:
40 minutes

START-TO-FINISH TIME:
60 to 65 minutes

MAKE AHEAD:
No

Lemon and Olive Oil Sauce

⅓ cup/75 ml olive oil

2½ tbsp fresh lemon juice

2 tsp grated lemon zest

1½ tsp kosher salt

¼ tsp freshly ground black pepper

1 lb/455 g fresh baby spinach

3 tbsp olive oil

Kosher salt

Freshly ground black pepper

1 tbsp plus 1 tsp minced garlic

10 to 12 oz/280 to 340 g Campari or cherry tomatoes, cut crosswise into ¼-in/6-mm slices

1 cup/260 g canned chickpeas, rinsed and drained well

½ cup/75 g pitted Kalamata olives, coarsely chopped

4 mild, firm white fish fillets, such as halibut or cod (6 to 7 oz/170 to 200 g each), about 1 in/2.5 cm thick

½ cup/80 g crumbled feta

¼ cup/15 g Toasted Bread Crumbs (page 12)

1. Arrange a rack in the middle of the oven and preheat to 375°F/190°C. Oil a 9-by-13-in/23-by-33-cm or another shallow 3-qt/2.8-L baking dish.

2. For the Lemon and Olive Oil Sauce: Whisk together the olive oil, lemon juice, lemon zest, salt, and pepper in a small nonreactive bowl. Set aside.

3. Put the spinach in a large bowl and toss with the olive oil. Season with salt and pepper and spread it on the bottom of the prepared baking dish. Sprinkle the garlic evenly over the spinach. Arrange the tomato slices over the spinach and scatter the chickpeas and olives over the vegetables. Pour half of the sauce over all.

4. Arrange the fish on top of the vegetables and drizzle the remaining sauce over the fillets. Sprinkle the feta over the fish and vegetables, and sprinkle some toasted bread crumbs on top of each fillet.

5. Bake, uncovered, until the fish is opaque and flakes easily and the spinach has wilted, 20 to 25 minutes, depending on the thickness of the fish. Serve immediately.

Salmon Baked with Spring Vegetables and Fresh Herbs

Everything about this dish—the fish, the herbs, and the vegetables—tastes fresh, and it all blends beautifully with a mustard-scented white sauce. You can prepare this casserole several hours ahead and will need only to place it in the oven for a few minutes at serving time. Add a watercress salad tossed in a citrus dressing to round out the meal.

Serves 4 to 5

PREP TIME:
25 minutes

START-TO-FINISH TIME:
1 hour, 15 minutes

MAKE AHEAD:
Yes

Herbed White Sauce
2 tbsp unsalted butter
2 tbsp all-purpose flour
2 cups/480 ml whole milk
1 tbsp Dijon mustard
½ tsp kosher salt
¼ tsp freshly ground black pepper
1 tbsp chopped fresh dill
1 tbsp chopped fresh mint

¾ cup/40 g Toasted Bread Crumbs (page 12)
1½ tsp grated lemon zest, plus 1 tbsp fresh
   lemon juice
One 1-lb/455-g salmon fillet (cut from the
   center section), about ¾ in/2 cm thick, skin
   removed (see Market Note)
1½ medium cucumbers
1½ cups/135 g sugar snap peas, ends
   trimmed, and halved on the diagonal
½ cup/70 g shelled fresh peas or frozen peas,
   defrosted
½ tsp kosher salt
¼ tsp freshly ground black pepper
1 tbsp chopped fresh dill
1 tbsp chopped fresh mint, plus a few sprigs
   (optional) for garnish

1. Arrange a rack in the middle of the oven and preheat to 400°F/200°C. Generously butter a 2-qt/2-L shallow baking dish.

2. For the Herbed White Sauce: Melt the butter until hot in a medium saucepan over medium heat. Add the flour and cook, stirring constantly, for 1½ to 2 minutes. Stir in the milk and bring to a gentle boil, whisking constantly until the mixture thickens enough to coat the back of a spoon, 6 to 8 minutes. Remove from the heat and stir in the mustard, salt, pepper, dill, and mint. Set aside to cool for about 10 minutes.

3. In a small bowl, toss the bread crumbs with half the lemon zest; cover and set aside.

4. Cut the salmon fillet into 1-in/2.5-cm chunks and put them in the prepared baking dish. Toss them with the lemon juice and the remaining lemon zest.

5. Peel the cucumbers and halve them lengthwise. Using a teaspoon, scoop out the seeds. Cut the halves crosswise into ½-in-/12-mm-thick slices.

6. Bring a large saucepan of water to a boil and add the cucumber and sugar snap peas, plus the peas if they are fresh. (Frozen peas do not need to be cooked.) Cook for 1 minute only, just to set the color, and drain the vegetables in a colander. Place under cold running water until the vegetables are cool. Pat them dry, and scatter them among the salmon cubes. Sprinkle the fish and vegetables with the salt, pepper, dill, and chopped mint and toss gently to mix.

7. Pour the cooled sauce over the fish and vegetables and spread evenly. (The casserole can be prepared up to this point 4 hours ahead; cover and refrigerate. Bring to room temperature 30 minutes before baking.)

8. Sprinkle the bread crumb mixture over the casserole. Bake, uncovered, until the salmon is cooked through (check with a sharp knife) and the vegetables are crisp-tender, 12 to 14 minutes.

9. Remove the casserole from the oven, and let stand for 5 minutes. If desired, garnish with mint sprigs before serving.

 MARKET NOTE:

When buying the salmon fillets, ask the fishmonger to remove the skin for you.

Cod and Red-Skin Potato Gratins

It's not often that a restaurant dish is so delicious and so simple that I can't wait to try it in my own kitchen. During a long stay in Paris, though, I was impressed by a casserole of roasted cod served atop gratinéed potatoes at a modest Left Bank bistro called Le Casse Noix (The Nutcracker). It was an unlikely combination, but it worked beautifully. Chef Pierre Olivier Lenormand had fashioned a delectable mixture of potatoes and bits of ham seasoned with *piment d'Espelette* (a Basque pepper similar to cayenne), and then transferred it to individual baking dishes. He sprinkled the servings with cheese, and finally added a thick, snowy white cod fillet to each one. After making this entrée several times, I returned to the restaurant and told the chef about my culinary attempts. He could not have been more charming, replying that my home version was close to the original.

Serves 4

PREP TIME:
10 minutes

START-TO-FINISH TIME:
50 minutes

MAKE AHEAD:
Partially

1¼ lb/570 g small red-skin or Yukon gold
  potatoes

2½ tsp dried thyme

1½ tsp kosher salt

¾ tsp cayenne pepper

3 thick strips bacon, cut crosswise into
  ½-in-/12-mm-wide pieces

½ cup/40 g grated Gruyère cheese

4 cod fillets (6 oz/170 g each), about 1 in/
  2.5 cm thick

½ cup/120 ml dry white wine

½ cup/120 ml reduced-sodium chicken broth

4 fresh thyme sprigs for garnish (optional)

1. Arrange a rack in the middle of the oven and preheat to 425°F/220°C. Generously butter four 5½-in/14-cm gratin or brûlée dishes and place on a rimmed baking sheet.

2. Bring a large saucepan of salted water to a boil. Peel the potatoes and slice ¼ in/6 mm thick. Cook the potatoes in the boiling water until tender but not mushy, 8 to 10 minutes. Drain in a colander.

3. Divide the potatoes evenly among the gratin dishes, in a single layer, overlapping the potatoes slightly. Combine ½ tsp of the thyme, ½ tsp of the salt, and ¼ tsp of the cayenne in a small bowl and sprinkle the potatoes with this mixture.

4. Sauté the bacon, stirring, in a medium, heavy frying pan over medium heat until crisp and browned, 4 to 5 minutes. Drain on paper towels. Sprinkle the bacon evenly over the potatoes and do the same with the Gruyère. (The potatoes can be prepared up to this point 4 hours ahead; cover with plastic wrap and leave at cool room temperature.)

5. Mix the remaining 2 tsp thyme, ½ tsp cayenne, and 1 tsp salt in a small bowl. Season the fish on both sides with this mixture. Top each dish of potatoes with a fillet. Combine the wine and chicken broth in a measuring cup and pour ¼ cup/60 ml over the fish and the potatoes in each dish.

6. Bake, uncovered, until the fish is opaque and flakes easily, the cheese has melted, and the potatoes are hot and bubbling, 12 to 15 minutes, depending on the thickness of the fish. Watch carefully so that the fish does not overcook and become dry. There will still be some liquid in the baking dishes, which will be delicious with the fish and potatoes. If desired, garnish with the thyme sprigs before serving.

MARKET VEGETABLES

Seasonal Sides and Centerpieces

"Keep it seasonal" is my mantra when making vegetable casseroles. The gratins, savory puddings, and layered creations in this chapter were inspired by the produce at my farmers' market and neighborhood groceries. In the summer, when tomatoes are abundant, try a Tian of Tomatoes and Summer Squash with Basil and Mint (page 95). In the fall and winter months, when heartier vegetables take center stage, you can turn to Swiss Chard, Mascarpone, and Cherry Tomato Gratin (page 90) or Fennel Halves au Gratin (page 103). And nothing says spring better than Creamed Peas and Spring Onions with Buttered Bread Crumbs (page 88), a light and verdant menu choice.

Some of these casseroles are ideal main courses, while others work best as sides to roasted, grilled, or sautéed meat, fish, or poultry. A rich vegetable moussaka makes an exceptionally satisfying meatless entrée, which will serve a crowd. My Baked "Risotto" with Butternut Squash, Sage, and Parmigiano (page 101) is cooked in the oven for ultimate convenience. Topped with sautéed prosciutto, this luscious centerpiece needs only a salad of mixed greens for an elegant meal. The Corn, Leek, and Chorizo Pudding (page 99) could be a perfect light supper, or a hearty side to pair with grilled steaks or chops. And Individual Broccoli and Cauliflower Cheddar Gratins (page 92) napped with a sharp cheese sauce would add real pizzazz to a simple roast chicken dinner.

Assembling these casseroles with the best and freshest ingredients is smart cooking—you'll save money by buying what's in season, and, of course, fresh produce will always surpass frozen or canned options in flavor.

Only Vegetables Moussaka

Like traditional moussaka, the famous Greek casserole of eggplant and lamb covered with a rich white sauce, this delicious vegetarian version will take a few hours to make and bake. You'll be rewarded, however, with a glorious main course, which can be completely assembled in advance. The dish, composed of layers of roasted eggplant cloaked with a fragrantly spiced tomato and portobello mushroom sauce, is topped with a luxurious béchamel enriched with cheese and eggs. Whenever I serve this casserole, my guests always say that the portobello mushrooms lend such a great meaty flavor to this moussaka that they don't miss the lamb at all!

Serves 8

PREP TIME:
1 hour, including 30 minutes for the eggplant to drain

START-TO-FINISH TIME:
3 hours, 30 minutes

MAKE AHEAD:
Yes

FREEZE:
Yes, before baking (see directions on page 11)

Eggplant and Mushroom Filling

3½ lb/1.6 kg eggplant, unpeeled, cut into ½-in-/12-mm-thick rounds

Kosher salt

½ cup/120 ml olive oil

1 large onion, halved and thinly sliced

1 cup/135 g finely chopped carrots

1 cup/115 g finely chopped celery

1 tbsp plus 1 tsp minced garlic

12 oz/340 g portobello mushrooms, stemmed, cleaned, and cut into ½-in/12-mm dice

1 tsp dried oregano

½ tsp ground cinnamon

One 28-oz/800-g can diced tomatoes, with their juices

¼ cup/10 g chopped fresh flat-leaf parsley

Freshly ground black pepper

1. For the Eggplant and Mushroom Filling: Cover two baking sheets with paper towels. Sprinkle both sides of the eggplant rounds with salt. Arrange in a single layer atop the towels and let stand 30 minutes.

2. Arrange racks in the upper and lower thirds of the oven and preheat to 425°F/220°C. Remove the eggplant and paper towels from the baking sheets and pat the eggplant dry. Oil the same baking sheets. Brush both sides of the eggplant rounds with ¼ cup/60 ml of the olive oil and arrange in a single layer on the baking sheets. Bake for 10 minutes, and then turn the eggplant and rotate the pans in the oven, top to bottom. Continue baking until the eggplant is tender, 10 to 15 minutes longer. Remove from the oven and set aside to cool.

3. Reduce the oven temperature to 350°F/180°C. Lightly oil a 9-by-13-in/23-by-33-cm or another shallow 3-qt/2.8-L baking dish.

4. Heat the remaining ¼ cup/60 ml oil in a large, heavy frying pan over medium-high heat. Add the onion, carrots, and celery and sauté until the onion is very tender, about 12 minutes. Mix in the garlic and add the mushrooms. Sauté until all the liquid from the mushrooms evaporates, 10 to 15 minutes. Stir in the oregano and cinnamon, and add the

tomatoes and parsley. Cook until the mixture thickens and most of the tomato juices have evaporated, about 10 minutes. Season the mixture with salt and several grinds of pepper. Set aside.

5. For the Extra-Rich White Sauce with Parmesan Cheese: Melt the butter in a large saucepan over medium heat. Add the flour and cook, stirring constantly, for 1½ to 2 minutes. Add the milk and bring to a gentle boil, whisking constantly until the mixture thickens enough to coat the back of a spoon, 4 to 5 minutes. Whisk in the Parmesan, and season the sauce with the salt, several grinds of pepper, and the nutmeg. Whisk the egg yolks in a large bowl to blend, and then gradually whisk in the hot sauce.

6. Arrange half of the eggplant rounds in a single layer in the prepared baking dish. Spoon half of the tomato mixture evenly over the eggplant, and sprinkle with 2 tbsp of the grated Parmesan. Repeat the layers with the remaining egg-plant and tomato mixture and 2 tbsp more of the cheese. Pour the sauce over the vegetables in the dish, and spread with a spatula. Sprinkle the remaining ¼ cup/30 g cheese over the sauce. (The moussaka can be made up to this point 1 day ahead; cool, cover, and refrigerate. Bring to room temperature 30 minutes before baking.)

7. Bake the moussaka, uncovered, until heated through and the sauce is golden brown on top, 45 to 55 minutes. Cool for 15 minutes before serving.

Extra-Rich White Sauce with Parmesan Cheese

6 tbsp/85 g unsalted butter

¼ cup plus 3 tbsp/55 g all-purpose flour

3½ cups/840 ml whole milk

½ cup/60 g grated Parmesan cheese,
   preferably Parmigiano-Reggiano

½ tsp kosher salt

Freshly ground black pepper

½ tsp freshly grated nutmeg

4 egg yolks

½ cup/60 g grated Parmesan cheese,
   preferably Parmigiano-Reggiano

Creamed Peas and Spring Onions with Buttered Bread Crumbs

Verdant harbingers of the season—peas, sugar snaps, and spring onions—are sautéed and then combined with julienned iceberg lettuce, which adds a subtle crispness to this casserole. A rich, creamy sauce scented with fresh herbs covers this vegetable medley while it bakes. I love the freshness and the elegance of this casserole, which could be served with roast lamb, baked ham, grilled salmon, and many other main courses.

Serves 6

PREP TIME:
15 minutes

START-TO-FINISH TIME:
1 hour, 10 minutes

MAKE AHEAD:
Yes

3 tbsp unsalted butter

1½ cups/130 g spring onions (white and light green parts only), sliced ¼ in/6 mm thick (see Market Note)

2¼ cups/315 g shelled fresh peas

2 cups/180 g trimmed and diagonally sliced sugar snap peas (1-in/2.5-cm slices)

¾ tsp sugar

1 small head iceberg lettuce

Kosher salt

Freshly ground pepper

White Sauce with Lemon and Spring Herbs

2 tbsp unsalted butter

2 tbsp all-purpose flour

1 cup/240 ml heavy or whipping cream

½ cup/120 ml whole milk

1 tbsp chopped fresh mint

1 tbsp chopped fresh tarragon

¾ tsp grated lemon zest

Kosher salt

Freshly ground black pepper

¾ cup/40 g Toasted Bread Crumbs (page 12), made with butter

1. Arrange a rack in the middle of the oven and preheat to 350°F/180°C. Generously butter a 2-qt/2-L baking dish.

2. Melt the butter in a medium, heavy frying pan over medium heat. When hot, add the spring onions and cook, stirring, until they just start to soften, about 3 minutes. Add the peas and sugar snap peas and cook, stirring often, until they are crisp-tender, about 4 minutes. Transfer the vegetables to a large bowl and sprinkle with the sugar. Set aside (but do not clean) the frying pan.

3. Quarter and core the head of lettuce. Slice each quarter into ¼-in-/6-mm-wide ribbons to yield 3 cups/210 g. (Save any extra lettuce for another use.) Add the lettuce ribbons to the bowl and toss to combine with the other vegetables. Season with salt and pepper.

4. For the White Sauce with Lemon and Spring Herbs: Set the frying pan in which you cooked the vegetables over low heat, and melt the butter. When hot, add the flour and cook, stirring, for 1½ to 2 minutes. Add the cream and milk and whisk until the mixture thickens and is smooth, 3 to 5 minutes. Stir in the mint, tarragon, lemon zest, and ½ tsp salt. Season with pepper and more salt, if needed. Set aside at cool room temperature for about 15 minutes.

5. Pour the cooled sauce over the vegetables and toss gently to combine. Spread the mixture evenly in the prepared baking dish. (The casserole can be prepared up to this point 4 hours ahead; cover and refrigerate. Bring to room temperature 30 minutes before continuing with the recipe.)

6. Sprinkle the bread crumbs over the casserole, and bake, uncovered, until the vegetables are hot, about 20 minutes. Serve immediately.

 MARKET NOTE:

Spring onions, as their name implies, are available in the spring. Like green onions, they have long green stems, but their white bulbs are larger, usually at least 1 in/2.5 cm in diameter. They have a more defined taste than green onions and work well in this dish. However, if you can't find them, substitute 1 cup/135 g frozen pearl onions. Defrost the frozen onions, and halve through the root ends. Sauté for about 3 minutes, until just starting to soften, before adding the peas and sugar snaps to the pan.

Swiss Chard, Mascarpone, and Cherry Tomato Gratin

When I was a youngster, turnip greens and collards were familiar staples at our table, but Swiss chard was never on the menu. Not until many years later did I discover this delicious, nutrient-packed, leafy green. In this recipe, the leaves and stems are sautéed, combined with creamy mascarpone and grated Parmesan, and then spooned into a dish for baking. Sliced cherry tomatoes tossed with a little balsamic vinegar make colorful accents to this tempting side.

Serves 6

PREP TIME:
25 minutes

START-TO-FINISH TIME:
1 hour, 5 minutes

MAKE AHEAD:
Yes

2½ lb/1.2 kg Swiss chard

3 tbsp olive oil

2 cups/250 g chopped onion

1 tbsp minced garlic

¾ tsp red pepper flakes

1 cup/240 ml mascarpone

¾ cup/90 g grated Parmesan,
   preferably Parmigiano-Reggiano

1⅛ tsp kosher salt

½ cup/90 g sliced cherry tomatoes

1 tsp balsamic vinegar

1. Arrange a rack in the middle of the oven and preheat to 375°F/190°C. Generously oil a 9-by-13-in/23-by-33-cm or another shallow 3-qt/2.8-L baking dish.

2. Cut the stems off the chard leaves and cut enough of the stems into small dice to equal 2 cups/225 g. Discard the rest. With a sharp knife, cut out the tough stems that run through the centers of the chard leaves and discard.

3. Fill a large saucepan two-thirds full with water and bring to a boil. Add the chard leaves and cook until wilted, only about 1 minute. Drain the chard and spin in a salad spinner to remove as much water as possible. (If you don't have a spinner, drain the chard in a colander, pressing down with the back of wooden spoon to extract as much liquid as possible.) Place the chard on a clean kitchen towel and wring out any remaining moisture. Chop coarsely.

4. Heat 1½ tbsp of the olive oil in a medium, heavy frying pan over medium heat. When hot, add the diced chard stems and onion; cook, stirring, until softened, about 4 minutes. Stir in the garlic and red pepper flakes and cook for 1 minute more. Transfer the mixture to a large bowl and add the chard leaves. Add the mascarpone and ½ cup/60 g of the Parmesan and stir until the cheeses are blended into the mixture. Season with 1 tsp of the salt.

5. Spread the chard mixture in the prepared baking dish. In a small bowl, toss the sliced tomatoes with balsamic vinegar and remaining ⅛ tsp salt and arrange them on the top of the chard. Sprinkle 2 tbsp of the remaining Parmesan over the casserole. (The gratin can be prepared up to this point 2 hours ahead; cool, cover, and refrigerate. Bring to room temperature 30 minutes before baking.)

6. Bake the casserole, uncovered, until hot and the cheese has melted, 15 to 20 minutes. Remove from the oven and sprinkle the remaining 2 tbsp Parmesan over the dish before serving.

Individual Broccoli and Cauliflower Cheddar Gratins

Broccoli and cauliflower, those winter staples, are far more interesting combined than when served alone. In this recipe, the tender florets, which are available fresh and conveniently packaged in many supermarkets, are arranged in individual baking dishes, and napped with a rich cheddar sauce, scented with lemon. These little gratins would make a distinctive side to roast chicken or leg of lamb, or just about any beef roast.

Serves 4

PREP TIME:
20 minutes

START-TO-FINISH TIME:
1 hour, 10 minutes

MAKE AHEAD:
Yes

Kosher salt

4 cups/430 g cauliflower florets

4 cups/240 g broccoli florets

1½ tbsp unsalted butter

1½ tbsp all-purpose flour

1½ cups/360 ml whole milk

1½ cups/150 g grated sharp white
    cheddar cheese

1½ tsp grated lemon zest

¾ tsp Dijon mustard

Pinch of cayenne pepper

2 tbsp Toasted Bread Crumbs (page 12)

1. Arrange a rack in the middle of the oven and preheat to 350°F/180°C. Generously butter four 5½-in/14-cm gratin or crème brûlée dishes and place on a rimmed baking sheet.

2. Add 2 tsp salt to a large saucepan of boiling water. Add the cauliflower and broccoli florets and cook until the vegetables are tender when pierced with a sharp knife, about 5 minutes. Drain in a colander under cold running water until the vegetables are cool, and pat dry.

3. Melt the butter in a medium saucepan over medium heat. When hot, add the flour and cook, stirring constantly, for 1½ to 2 minutes. Gradually pour in the milk and whisk constantly until the sauce thickens and comes to a gentle boil, 5 to 6 minutes. Gradually whisk in 1¼ cups/125 g of the cheddar, the lemon zest, mustard, ½ tsp salt, and the cayenne. Season with more salt if needed.

4. Alternate the broccoli and cauliflower florets in single layers in each gratin dish and salt lightly. (You may have extra florets, depending on the size of your dishes.) Pour one-fourth of the sauce over the vegetables in each dish. (The gratins can be prepared up to this point 3 hours ahead; cool, cover, and refrigerate. Bring to room temperature before continuing with the recipe.)

continued . . .

5. Sprinkle the top of each gratin with 1 tbsp of the remaining cheddar and 1½ tsp of the bread crumbs. Bake the gratins until the cheese has melted on the top and the vegetables are hot, about 15 minutes. Remove from the oven and cool for 5 minutes before serving.

COOKING TIP:

You can make this recipe in a single dish. Use a 9-by-13-in/23-by-33-cm or another shallow 3-qt/2.8-L baking dish. Arrange the vegetables in a single layer. Proceed with the recipe and bake for about 30 minutes.

Tian of Tomatoes and Summer Squash with Basil and Mint

A Provençal specialty, a tian is composed of layers of vegetables, which are baked together in a casserole. As the vegetables cook, their flavors meld, resulting in a mouthwatering combination of textures and tastes. In this recipe, I used that triumvirate of summer produce—zucchini, yellow squash, and tomatoes—and added fresh herbal accents. A sprinkle of snowy white feta and toasted bread crumbs completes the dish. You can serve this casserole as a side to grilled lamb or chicken, or make it the star attraction, accompanied by a salad and a warm baguette.

Serves 4 as a main course, or 6 as a side dish

PREP TIME:
30 minutes

START-TO-FINISH TIME:
1 hour, 45 minutes

MAKE AHEAD:
Yes

1¼ lb/570 g zucchini, ends trimmed, and sliced into ¼-in/6-mm rounds

1¼ lb/570 g yellow squash, ends trimmed, and sliced into ¼-in/6-mm rounds

Kosher salt

Freshly ground black pepper

½ cup plus 1 tbsp/135 ml olive oil

1½ cups/190 g chopped onion

1 tbsp minced garlic

3 lb/1.4 kg ripe tomatoes, cut crosswise into ¼-in-/6-mm-thick rounds

3 tbsp finely chopped fresh basil

3 tbsp finely chopped fresh mint

1 cup/170 g crumbled feta cheese

⅓ cup/20 g Toasted Bread Crumbs (page 12)

1. Arrange racks in the upper and lower thirds of the oven and preheat to 425°F/220°C. Generously oil two baking sheets and a 9-by-13-in/23-by-33-cm or another shallow 3-qt/2.8-L baking dish.

2. Arrange the zucchini in a single layer on one baking sheet and the yellow squash on another, and season both generously with salt and pepper. Drizzle 2 tbsp of the olive oil over the zucchini and 2 tbsp more over the yellow squash. Put the baking sheets in the oven and bake for 10 minutes. With a metal spatula, turn the zucchini and squash, and rotate the baking sheets, top to bottom. Continue to roast until the zucchini and squash are tender when pierced with a knife and are lightly browned on the bottom, 12 to 15 minutes. Remove the baking sheets from the oven.

3. Heat 2 tbsp of the olive oil in a medium, heavy frying pan over medium heat. When hot, add the onion and cook, stirring, until softened, 3 to 4 minutes. Add the garlic and cook, stirring, for 1 minute more. Season with ¼ tsp salt and several grinds of pepper.

continued . . .

4. Arrange all the zucchini in a single layer in the prepared baking dish. Spread half the onion mixture on top. Cover with half of the tomatoes. Season with the salt and pepper and sprinkle with one-third of the basil and mint and half of the feta. Repeat the layers, this time beginning with a layer of all the yellow squash to cover the feta. You should have about 1 tbsp of basil and 1 tbsp of mint left over. (The casserole can be prepared to this point 3 hours ahead; cover and refrigerate. Bring the casserole to room temperature 30 minutes before baking. Wrap the remaining basil and mint in a wet paper towel and leave at room temperature.)

5. Sprinkle the bread crumbs over the top layer, and drizzle with the remaining 3 tbsp olive oil. Bake, uncovered, for 20 minutes, and then lower the heat to 350°F/180°C. Continue baking until the vegetables are tender when pierced with a sharp knife and the feta is lightly browned, about 15 minutes.

6. Remove the casserole from the oven and cool for 15 minutes. Sprinkle the remaining basil and mint over the tian before serving.

Golden Scalloped Potatoes with Camembert

When I came across a French recipe for scalloped potatoes baked with Camembert cheese, I couldn't wait to try it. The sauce was cleverly prepared by melting small cubes of Camembert (rind and all) in cream, and then it was poured over layers of sliced potatoes. Nothing could be simpler or more delicious. Serve this casserole as an accompaniment to your favorite roast, or try it alongside grilled chops or steaks, but don't be surprised if it upstages the main course!

Serves 4 to 6

PREP TIME:
15 minutes

START-TO-FINISH TIME:
1 hour, 30 minutes

MAKE AHEAD:
No

1⅓ cups/315 ml half-and-half, or ⅔ cup/ 165 ml heavy cream and ⅔ cup/165 ml whole milk

6 oz/170 g Camembert cheese, with the rind, cut into ½-in/12-mm dice

Pinch of freshly grated nutmeg

Pinch of cayenne pepper

Kosher salt

2 lb/910 g Yukon gold potatoes, peeled and cut crosswise into ⅛-in-/3-mm-thick rounds

Freshly ground black pepper

1 tbsp plus 1 tsp chopped fresh flat-leaf parsley

1. Arrange a rack in the middle of the oven and preheat to 375°F/190°C. Generously butter a 2- to 2½-qt/2- to 2.4-L shallow baking dish.

2. Pour the half-and-half into a medium saucepan over medium heat and bring to a simmer. Reduce the heat to low and add two-thirds of the diced Camembert. Stir until the cheese has melted, 2 to 3 minutes. (The sauce will be smooth but have little bits of rind floating in it; that's okay.) Stir in the nutmeg and cayenne, and remove the saucepan from the heat. Season with salt if needed.

3. Arrange half of the potato slices in a single layer in the prepared baking dish, overlapping them, and salt and pepper generously. Ladle half of the sauce over the potatoes and spread it evenly with a spatula. Repeat to make a second layer of potatoes covered with sauce. Season with salt and pepper.

4. Bake the potatoes, uncovered, for 15 minutes, and then reduce the heat to 350°F/180°C. Bake for 30 minutes more. Sprinkle the remaining diced Camembert over the top of the potatoes, and continue baking until the potatoes are tender when pierced with a sharp knife and the cheese on top has melted to a golden brown, about 15 minutes. Remove from the oven and cool for 5 minutes.

5. Sprinkle the potatoes with the parsley before serving.

Corn, Leek, and Chorizo Pudding

In the summer when, as those famous lyrics go, corn is as "high as an elephant's eye," this is the perfect dish to make. After baking, this savory pudding boasts a golden crust, which covers a creamy custard studded with a mosaic of fresh corn kernels, bits of chorizo, and chopped leeks. The casserole could be served as a main course, along with a salad, or offered as a side for grilled chicken or steaks.

Serves 8 as a side dish, 4 as a main course

PREP TIME:
30 minutes

START-TO-FINISH TIME:
1 hour, 15 minutes

MAKE AHEAD:
Yes

3 tbsp olive oil, plus more if needed

8 oz/225 g Spanish chorizo, cut into
 ½-in/12-mm cubes (see Market Note)

5 cups/725 g fresh corn kernels
 (8 to 10 large ears)

2 cups/160 g chopped leeks (white and light
 green parts only, 3 to 4 medium leeks)

4 large eggs

1½ cups/360 ml half-and-half

½ cup/120 ml sour cream

1½ cups/120 g grated Gruyère cheese

2 tbsp chopped fresh flat-leaf parsley,
 plus 1 or 2 sprigs for garnish

½ tsp kosher salt

¼ tsp freshly ground black pepper

MARKET NOTE:

Chorizo is a highly seasoned pork sausage used in Spanish and Mexican cuisines. Spanish chorizo, which is used in this recipe, is made with smoked pork and is already cooked. Mexican chorizo is prepared with fresh pork. Larger markets, including Whole Foods, often sell the Spanish variety.

1. Arrange a rack in the middle of the oven and preheat to 350°F/180°C. Generously butter a 9-by-13-in/23-by-33-cm or another shallow 3-qt/2.8-L baking dish.

2. Heat the olive oil in a large, heavy frying pan over medium heat. When hot, add the chorizo and sauté until lightly browned, 3 to 4 minutes. Remove with a slotted spoon and drain on paper towels. Add the corn and leeks to the same frying pan. Cook, stirring often and adding more oil if needed, until the corn and leeks are softened, 8 to 10 minutes. Cool for 5 minutes.

3. In a large bowl, whisk the eggs, half-and-half, and sour cream together. Add the chorizo, the corn mixture, 1 cup/80 g of the Gruyère, and the chopped parsley and mix well. Stir in the salt and pepper. Transfer this mixture to the prepared baking dish and sprinkle with the remaining ½ cup/40 g Gruyère.

4. Bake the casserole, uncovered, until the top is golden and a knife inserted into the center comes out clean, about 35 minutes. Remove from the oven and let stand for 10 minutes. (The pudding can be prepared 6 hours ahead; cool, cover, and refrigerate. Bring to room temperature, and reheat in a preheated 350°F/180°C until hot, 15 to 20 minutes.) Garnish the center of the pudding with parsley sprigs before serving.

Baked "Risotto" with Butternut Squash, Sage, and Parmigiano

I adore risotto, but I rarely make it for company since it requires a good deal of cooking at the last minute. Recently, though, I've discovered that baking risotto in a casserole is stress free. Arborio rice is spread in a baking dish, covered with hot simmering broth and melted butter, and placed in a hot oven, where the liquids are absorbed by the grains. Cooked this way, like a pilaf, the rice is tender, rather than al dente and creamy, as in classic risotto. The addition of roasted butternut squash, grated Parmigiano, and fresh sage make this baked version even better.

Serves 6 as a side dish, or 4 as a main course

PREP TIME:
20 minutes, including peeling and cubing the squash

START-TO-FINISH TIME:
1 hour, 15 minutes

MAKE AHEAD:
Yes

3 cups/450 g peeled diced butternut squash
  (¾-in/2-cm dice; see Market Note)

3 tbsp olive oil

Kosher salt

Freshly ground black pepper

1½ cups/315 g Arborio rice

3¾ cups/900 ml reduced-sodium chicken broth

3 tbsp unsalted butter

1½ oz/40 g thinly sliced prosciutto, cut into strips about ¼ in/6 mm wide and 3 in/7.5 cm long

1 cup/120 g grated Parmesan cheese, preferably Parmigiano-Reggiano

1½ tbsp chopped fresh sage, plus 3 or 4 sprigs for garnish

1. Arrange racks in the center and lower third of the oven, and preheat to 375°F/190°C. Generously butter a shallow 2-qt/2-L baking dish and have two rimmed baking sheets ready.

2. Spread the squash on one of the baking sheets, and toss with 2 tbsp of the olive oil. Season with ½ tsp salt and several grinds of pepper.

3. Spread the rice in the prepared baking dish and place the dish on the other baking sheet. Heat the chicken broth and butter in a large saucepan over medium-high heat until the broth comes to a boil. Carefully pour the hot broth over the rice. Cover the baking dish tightly with foil.

4. Place the baking sheet with the rice on the middle oven rack and the one with the squash on the lower rack. Roast the squash, stirring every 10 minutes, until it is soft when pierced with a sharp knife and golden brown around the edges, about 35 minutes. At the same time, cook the rice until all the liquid has been absorbed, about 40 minutes.

continued . . .

5. While the rice and squash are in the oven, heat the remaining 1 tbsp olive oil in a small frying pan over medium-high heat, and sauté the prosciutto, stirring often, until crisp, about 2 minutes. Remove from the pan and drain on paper towels.

6. When done, remove the squash and the risotto from the oven. Carefully remove the foil from the baking dish and stir in ½ cup/60 g of the Parmesan cheese and the chopped sage. Gently stir in the roasted butternut squash. Season with salt and pepper if desired. (The risotto can be prepared 30 minutes ahead. Keep, loosely covered with foil, at room temperature.)

7. Garnish the center of the risotto with the sage sprigs and sprinkle with the sautéed prosciutto. Serve the risotto with a small bowl of the remaining Parmesan cheese for sprinkling.

 MARKET NOTE:

Butternut squash can often be purchased already peeled (a big time-saver). If you are buying it this way, you'll need about 1 lb/455 g of peeled squash.

Fennel Halves au Gratin

I've tried countless recipes for fennel, that Mediterranean staple that tastes slightly of licorice, but none that I like better than this one. Halved fennel bulbs are blanched, set upon a bed of sautéed onions and crispy bacon, and then topped with crème fraîche and cheddar. Luxuriously rich, this delectable casserole can be assembled several hours ahead. It would make a special side to simple entrées, such as baked ham, roast leg of lamb, or grilled salmon.

Serves 8

PREP TIME:
20 minutes

START-TO-FINISH TIME:
1 hour, 15 minutes

MAKE AHEAD:
Yes

4 medium fennel bulbs, 3 in/7.5 cm wide at the base

Kosher salt

5 bacon slices, cut into 1-in/2.5-cm pieces

2 tbsp olive oil

2 cups/260 g chopped onion

½ cup/120 ml crème fraîche, homemade (see page 12) or store-bought

½ cup/50 g grated sharp white cheddar cheese

2 tsp chopped fresh flat-leaf parsley

1. Arrange a rack in the middle of the oven and preheat to 400°F/200°C. Generously butter a shallow 2½- to 3-qt/ 2.4- to 2.8-L baking dish that will hold the halved fennel bulbs comfortably in a single layer.

2. Trim any lacy stems from the fennel bulbs, and halve the bulbs lengthwise. Cut out the tough triangular center core from each half. Bring a large pot of water to a boil and add 1 tbsp salt. Add the fennel and cook at a simmer until tender when pierced with a sharp knife, 15 to 20 minutes. Remove with a slotted spoon to a colander to drain, and discard the cooking water. (If the fennel halves separated during cooking, don't worry; you can reassemble them into halves after they have been drained.)

3. While the fennel is cooking, sauté the bacon pieces in a large, heavy frying pan over medium heat until browned and crisp. Remove and drain on paper towels. Discard the drippings in the pan and add the olive oil. When hot, add the onion and cook, stirring, until softened and lightly browned, 6 to 7 minutes.

continued . . .

4. Spread the onion in the bottom of the prepared baking dish and sprinkle two-thirds of the bacon over it. Arrange the fennel bulbs, cut-side up, in the dish and season lightly with salt. Spoon the crème fraîche over the fennel halves and sprinkle the halves with the cheddar. (The casserole can be prepared up to this point 6 hours ahead. Cover and refrigerate. Bring to room temperature 30 minutes before continuing with the recipe.)

5. Bake the gratin, uncovered, until hot and the cheese is beginning to brown, 25 to 30 minutes.

6. Crumble the remaining bacon and sprinkle it over the gratin, followed by the parsley, before serving.

CASSEROLES UNDER COVER

Biscuit, Potato, Cornmeal, and Pastry Toppings

Adding a topping—whether it's a butter-rich pastry, a mound of creamy whipped potatoes, a layer of golden cornbread, or flaky biscuits—makes a good casserole even better. Such additions add both flavor and texture to baked dishes. You'll need to spend extra time to assemble these "covers," but they will be well worth your effort.

In this chapter, cheese-studded pastry rounds cover individual chicken pot pies as well as a large smoked sausage and kale cottage pie. When baked, the crusts are irresistibly flaky and a perfect foil for the fillings beneath. For a Greek-style Lamb and Spinach Phyllo Pie (page 122), a lamb and fresh spinach filling is encased in multiple layers of phyllo, which bake to a golden crispness. Equally tempting is Chipotle Chili Baked Under a Cornbread Crust (page 119), a spicy chili covered with a cornbread batter, and then popped in the oven so that both chili and cornbread cook at the same time. No matter where he is in our house, when this dish comes out of the oven, my husband magically appears in the kitchen, ready for a sample.

Two variations on shepherd's pie—a salmon and fresh corn duo for summer and an orange-scented turkey and cranberry version for all those Thanksgiving leftovers—are both topped with mounds of whipped potatoes.

For me, there is something special about breaking through the topping of a covered casserole and discovering the tasty morsels underneath. I hope that these covered dishes with their delectable, hidden interiors will find their way into your casserole repertoire.

Chicken Pot Pies with Fall Vegetables and Golden Cheddar Crusts

If asked to choose a favorite from the hit parade of American comfort foods, chicken pot pies would top my list. The made-from-scratch pies featured here, though, are far different from the store-bought ones of my childhood. The filling, prepared with tender morsels of chicken, sautéed butternut squash, Brussels sprouts, and mushrooms, all enrobed in a smooth white sauce, is spooned into ramekins, then covered with cheese-flecked pastry rounds. When baked, the golden crusts are tender and flaky, a perfect contrast to the creamy chicken and vegetables beneath.

Serves 6

PREP TIME:
45 minutes

START-TO-FINISH TIME:
2 hours, 15 minutes

MAKE AHEAD:
Yes

FREEZE:
Yes, before baking
(see directions on
page 11)

Golden Cheddar Crust

3 cups/385 g sifted all-purpose flour

1 cup/100 g grated sharp white cheddar
   cheese

¾ cup/170 g cold unsalted butter, diced

4½ tbsp/60 g vegetable shortening, chilled
   and broken into small pieces

¾ tsp salt

¼ cup plus 2 tbsp/90 ml ice water

Chicken and Fall Vegetable Filling

2 tbsp unsalted butter

2 tbsp canola oil

1½ cups/215 g diced butternut squash
   (½-in/12-mm dice)

4 oz/115 g small Brussels sprouts, bases
   trimmed, and quartered lengthwise

4 oz/115 g small brown mushrooms (cremini)
   cut into ¼-in-/6-mm-thick slices

½ cup/55 g thinly sliced leeks (white and
   light green parts only)

1½ tsp crushed dried rosemary
   (see Market Note on page 34)

½ tsp kosher salt

1. For the Golden Cheddar Crust: Combine the flour, cheddar, butter, shortening, and salt in a food processor and pulse for 15 seconds. Add the ice water and process until a loose ball of dough forms, about 30 seconds. (If you have a small-capacity processor, divide the ingredients in half and make the dough in two batches.) Remove the dough and shape it into two equal balls. Flatten each one, wrap in plastic wrap, and refrigerate for 45 minutes.

2. For the Chicken and Fall Vegetable Filling: In a medium, heavy frying pan over medium heat, melt the butter with the canola oil until hot. Add the butternut squash and Brussels sprouts and sauté, stirring, for 3 minutes. Add the mushrooms and cook, stirring, for 3 minutes more. Add the leeks, rosemary, salt, and several grinds of pepper and cook, stirring, until the vegetables are lightly browned and just tender, about 2 minutes. Transfer the vegetables to a large bowl and add the chicken.

3. Arrange a rack in the middle of the oven and preheat to 375°F/190°C. Have ready six 1-cup/240-ml ramekins and a rimmed baking sheet.

4. For the White Sauce: Melt the butter in a medium saucepan over medium heat. When hot, add the flour and cook, stirring constantly, for 1½ to 2 minutes. Add the milk, ¾ tsp salt, and ⅛ tsp pepper and bring to a gentle boil, whisking constantly until the mixture thickens enough to coat the back of a spoon, about 5 minutes. Pour the sauce into the bowl with the chicken and vegetables and toss gently to combine. Season with salt and pepper if needed. Divide the mixture evenly among the ramekins.

5. On a floured surface, roll out one ball of dough to a circle about 11 in/28 cm in diameter and ¼ in/6 mm thick. Cut out three rounds that are 2 in/5 cm larger in diameter than the tops of the ramekins. (For example, if your ramekins are 4 in/10 cm in diameter, you would cut out 6-in/15-cm rounds.) You may need to gather the dough scraps and roll them out again to get three rounds. Repeat with the remaining ball of dough.

6. Brush a ½-in/12-mm border around the edge of each round with some of the beaten egg (this will help the pastry topping to adhere to the ramekin). Cover each ramekin with a circle of dough (egg-brushed-side down), and press the overhanging dough against the sides. Make a 1-in/2.5-cm slit in the center of each crust. (The pot pies can be prepared up to this point 1 day ahead. Cover each with plastic wrap and refrigerate. Bring to room temperature 30 minutes to 1 hour before baking. Cover and refrigerate the remaining beaten egg and whisk lightly before using.)

7. Place the pot pies on the rimmed baking sheet, and brush the pastry tops and sides with the remaining beaten egg. Bake until the tops are golden, 30 to 35 minutes (or slightly longer if the pies have been refrigerated). Remove from the oven and cool for 5 minutes before serving.

Freshly ground black pepper

2 cups/280 g diced cooked chicken or turkey (½-in/12-mm dice; see Market Note)

White Sauce

5 tbsp/70 g unsalted butter

¼ cup/30 g all-purpose flour

2½ cups/600 ml whole milk

Kosher salt

Freshly ground black pepper

1 large egg, lightly beaten

 MARKET NOTE:

You can use leftover chicken or turkey or buy a rotisserie bird. If you choose the latter, count on using more than half of the chicken.

 COOKING TIP:

To make the dough by hand, mix the flour, Cheddar, and salt together in a bowl. Cut in the butter and shortening with a pastry blender or two table knives until the mixture resembles oatmeal flakes. Gradually add the water, mixing just until the dough holds together.

Creamed Chicken, Apples, and Walnuts with a Biscuit Topping

Old-fashioned and homey, this chicken and biscuits casserole gets updated with the addition of sautéed apple slices and toasted walnuts. You can prepare the delicious creamed filling several hours ahead, and measure the ingredients for the biscuits in advance so that they can be quickly assembled at baking time.

Serves 4

PREP TIME:
25 minutes

START-TO-FINISH TIME:
1 hour, 25 minutes

MAKE AHEAD:
Yes, partially

Creamed Chicken and Apples

5½ tbsp/80 g unsalted butter

¼ cup/30 g all-purpose flour

1⅓ cups/315 ml whole milk

1⅓ cups/315 ml reduced-sodium chicken broth

⅔ cup/70 g grated sharp white cheddar cheese

1½ tsp Dijon mustard

Kosher salt

½ tsp Spanish smoked paprika (see Market Note on page 70)

⅛ tsp freshly grated nutmeg

Generous pinch of cayenne pepper

2 medium Golden Delicious apples, unpeeled, cored, and cut into ¼-in-/6-mm-thick slices

3 cups/420 g cubed cooked chicken (1-in/12-mm pieces; see Market Note)

½ cup/55 g walnuts, toasted and coarsely chopped (see page 12)

3 tbsp chopped fresh flat-leaf parsley

1. Arrange a rack in the middle of the oven and preheat to 400°F/200°C. Generously butter a 2-qt/2-L shallow baking dish.

2. For the Creamed Chicken and Apples: Melt 4 tbsp/55 g of the butter in a heavy, medium saucepan over medium heat. When hot, add the flour and cook, stirring constantly, for 1½ to 2 minutes. Add the milk and chicken broth and bring to a gentle boil, whisking until the mixture thickens enough to coat the back of a spoon, 3 to 4 minutes. Whisk in the cheddar, a little at a time, and continue whisking until the sauce is smooth. Remove the pan from the heat and stir in the mustard, ½ tsp salt, the smoked paprika, nutmeg, and cayenne.

3. In a large, heavy frying pan over medium heat, melt the remaining 1½ tbsp butter. When hot, add the apple slices. Cook, stirring, until slightly softened and just starting to turn golden, about 3 minutes. Stir the apples into the sauce and add the chicken, walnuts, and parsley. Season with salt if needed. Spoon the mixture into the prepared baking dish and spread evenly with a spatula. (The casserole can be prepared up to this point 3 hours ahead; cover and refrigerate. Bring to room temperature 1 hour before baking.)

4. For the Biscuits: Combine the flour, baking powder, and salt in a food processor and pulse, just to blend, for 30 seconds. Add the shortening and process until the mixture is crumbly, 30 to 40 seconds more. Transfer the mixture to a medium bowl and stir well to blend.

5. In a small bowl, whisk together the ½ cup/120 ml milk and mustard and add to the flour mixture. Stir just until all the flour is moistened. Remove the dough from the bowl and, with floured hands, knead gently and quickly on a lightly floured work surface, shaping it into a ball.

6. Roll out the dough into a circle about 7 in/17 cm in diameter and ¾ in/2 cm thick. With a 2-in/5-cm cookie cutter, cut out rounds. Reshape the scraps, roll out again, and cut out more rounds. You should get about twelve biscuits. Arrange them on top of the creamed chicken with a little space around each one. Brush the tops with the remaining 1 tbsp milk.

7. Bake until the biscuits have risen and the tops are golden, 18 to 20 minutes. If the biscuits are done but not browned, turn the oven to broil for 1 or 2 minutes. Serve warm.

Biscuits

2 cups/255 g all-purpose flour

1 tbsp baking powder

½ tsp salt

6 tbsp/85 g vegetable shortening, chilled and broken into small pieces

½ cup/120 ml whole milk, plus 1 tbsp

2 tbsp coarse-grain Dijon mustard

 **MARKET NOTE:**

You can use leftover chicken or buy a rotisserie bird. If you choose the latter, count on using the whole chicken.

COOKING TIP:

To make biscuit dough by hand, combine the flour, baking powder, and salt in a mixing bowl and stir well to blend. Add the shortening and, using a pastry blender or table knives, cut it into the flour until the mixture is crumbly. Stir in the milk and mustard.

After Thanksgiving, Turkey Shepherd's Pie

When you've made countless turkey sandwiches and are looking for something more creative to do with the leftover Thanksgiving bird, try this delicious shepherd's pie. For the filling, you simply combine sliced turkey with a quickly made brown sauce scented with orange and enriched with sautéed pearl onions and dried cranberries. Creamy mashed potatoes are spread over the turkey before the dish is popped in the oven.

Serves 4

PREP TIME:
25 minutes

START-TO-FINISH TIME:
1 hour, 30 minutes

MAKE AHEAD:
Yes

Turkey and Cranberry Filling

3½ tbsp/50 g unsalted butter

1 tbsp canola oil

1 cup/135 g frozen pearl onions, defrosted and patted dry

2½ tbsp all-purpose flour

1½ cups/360 ml reduced-sodium chicken broth

¼ cup/60 ml white wine

Heaping ⅓ cup/45 g dried cranberries

1¼ tsp grated orange zest

1 tsp dried thyme

Kosher salt

Freshly ground black pepper

1 lb/455 g cooked turkey, sliced about ¼ in/6 mm thick (see Cooking Tip)

1. Arrange a rack in the middle of the oven and preheat to 375°F/190°C. Generously butter a shallow 1½-qt/1.4-L baking dish.

2. For the Turkey and Cranberry Filling: Melt 1 tbsp of the butter with the canola oil in a heavy, medium saucepan over medium heat. When hot, add the pearl onions and sauté, stirring frequently, until nicely browned and tender when pierced with a sharp knife, 4 to 5 minutes. Remove from the saucepan and set aside.

3. In the same saucepan over medium heat, melt the remaining 2½ tbsp butter and, when hot, add the flour and whisk constantly until it turns medium brown, 2 to 3 minutes. Gradually add the chicken broth and bring to a gentle boil, whisking constantly until the sauce thickens enough to coat the back of a spoon. Stir in the wine, cranberries, orange zest, thyme, ½ tsp salt, and several grinds of pepper. Return the sautéed pearl onions to the pan. Cook for 1 minute more, and then remove from the heat and season with more salt if needed.

4. Either cut or tear the sliced turkey into strips about 3 in/ 7.5 cm long and ½ in/12 mm wide, and spread in the prepared baking dish. Pour the sauce over the turkey and toss well to coat evenly. (The casserole can be prepared up to this point 2 hours ahead. Cool, cover, and refrigerate. Bring to room temperature 30 minutes before continuing with the recipe.)

5. For the Mashed Potato Topping: Bring a large pot of water to a boil and add 1 tbsp salt. Cook the potatoes until tender, about 15 minutes. Heat the half-and-half and butter in a small saucepan until warm and set aside.

6. When the potatoes are done, drain them in a colander and return to the pot. Mash with a potato masher. Stir in the half-and-half and butter. Season the potatoes with ½ tsp salt, or more if needed. With a rubber or metal spatula, spread the mashed potatoes evenly on top of the turkey in the baking dish. Make wavy patterns in the potatoes with the spatula. (The casserole can be prepared up to this point 30 minutes ahead. Leave, uncovered, at cool room temperature.)

7. Bake the casserole, uncovered, until the potatoes are hot, about 15 minutes. Arrange a rack 4 to 5 in/10 to 12 cm from the broiler and broil the casserole, watching constantly, until the potatoes start to brown, 1 to 3 minutes. Remove from the oven and garnish, if desired, with a few thyme sprigs before serving.

Mashed Potato Topping

Kosher salt

1½ lb/680 g Yukon gold potatoes, peeled and cut into 1-in/2.5-cm cubes

¾ cup/180 ml half-and-half

1½ tbsp unsalted butter

Freshly ground black pepper

Fresh thyme sprigs for garnish (optional)

COOKING TIP:

You can use white or dark meat, but I particularly like white meat in this dish.

Smoked Sausage, Kale, and Mushroom Cottage Pie

This golden-crusted savory pie is the creation of my longtime assistant Emily Bell, who frequently goes on walking tours in the English countryside. Meals at picturesque inns along the routes are a highlight and often include warm cottage pies filled with sausages and vegetables, just like this one. This dish is quite rich, so simply add a mixed green salad with thinly sliced apples or pears tossed in a vinaigrette as a side or second course.

Serves 4

PREP TIME:
25 minutes

START-TO-FINISH TIME:
2 hours

MAKE AHEAD:
Yes

FREEZE:
Yes, before baking (see directions on page 11)

Dijon Mustard White Sauce

1 tbsp plus 1 tsp unsalted butter

2 tbsp all-purpose flour

1 cup/240 ml reduced-sodium chicken broth

⅓ cup/75 ml half-and-half

1½ tsp coarse-grain Dijon mustard

Potato, Sausage, and Kale Filling

Kosher salt

12 oz/340 g small Yukon gold potatoes

2 tbsp olive oil, plus more if needed

6 to 7 oz/170 to 200 g smoked sausage, such as kielbasa, halved lengthwise and cut into ½-in-/12-mm-thick slices

1 cup/135 g frozen pearl onions, defrosted and patted dry

6 oz/170 g small brown mushrooms (cremini), stemmed and quartered

8 oz/225 g kale, tough stems and center ribs removed, and leaves cut into ½-in-/12-mm-wide strips

Freshly ground black pepper

1. Arrange a rack in the middle of the oven and preheat to 375°F/190°C. Generously butter a 2-qt/2-L shallow baking dish.

2. For the Dijon Mustard White Sauce: Melt the butter in a medium saucepan over medium heat. When hot, add the flour and cook, stirring constantly, for 1½ to 2 minutes. Pour in the chicken broth and half-and-half, and whisk into the flour mixture. Bring to a gentle boil, whisking constantly until the mixture thickens enough to coat the back of a spoon, 3 to 4 minutes. Stir in the mustard and set aside.

3. For the Potato, Sausage, and Kale Filling: Bring a large saucepan of water to a boil and add 1 tbsp salt. Cook the potatoes until barely tender, 10 to 15 minutes. Drain well. Halve the potatoes, and cut each half in quarters. Set aside.

4. Heat the olive oil in a large, heavy frying pan over medium heat. When hot, add the sausage and sauté, stirring, for 3 minutes. Add the pearl onions and mushrooms, and more oil if needed. Sauté this mixture, stirring often, until the vegetables and sausage start to brown lightly, 3 to 4 minutes. Add half the kale and cook, stirring, until it wilts, about 2 minutes. Add the remaining kale and cook, stirring, until it has wilted, about 2 minutes more. Add the potatoes, white sauce, ½ tsp salt, and ¼ tsp pepper and combine well. Season with more salt and pepper if needed. Remove the filling from the pan and spread evenly in the prepared baking dish.

continued . . .

5. For the Cheddar Cheese Crust: Combine the flour, cheddar, and salt in the bowl of a food processor. Pulse several times to combine. Add the butter and shortening and pulse several times, until the mixture resembles coarse meal. With the machine running, add 2 tbsp ice water and gradually add up to another 2 tbsp ice water, stopping when the mixture starts to clump but has not formed a ball of dough.

6. Remove the dough to a floured work surface. Gather it into a ball, flatten it slightly, and roll it into a circle about 10 in/25 cm in diameter and ⅜ in/1 cm thick. Using a 2-in/5-cm round cookie cutter, cut circles from the dough. Gather the scraps into a ball, roll out again, and cut out more circles until all the dough has been used. Arrange the circles, slightly overlapping, to cover the top of the filling. (The casserole can be prepared up to this point 6 hours ahead; cover and refrigerate. Bring to room temperature 30 minutes to 1 hour before baking.)

7. When ready to bake, brush the dough with some of the beaten egg. Bake until the crust is golden and the filling is hot, 40 to 45 minutes. Remove from the oven and cool for 5 minutes before serving.

Cheddar Cheese Crust

1¼ cups/145 g all-purpose flour

½ cup/50 g grated sharp white
  cheddar cheese

¼ tsp salt

6 tbsp/85 g cold unsalted butter, diced

2 tbsp vegetable shortening, chilled and
  broken into small pieces

2 to 4 tbsp ice water

1 large egg, beaten well

COOKING TIP:

To make the dough by hand, mix the flour, cheese, and salt together in a bowl. Cut in the butter and shortening with a pastry blender or two table knives until the mixture resembles oatmeal flakes. Gradually add the water, mixing just until the dough holds together.

Chipotle Chili Baked Under a Cornbread Crust

Although prepared with the usual suspects—ground beef, onions, beans, and seasonings, including a generous kick of heat from chipotle chile powder—this chili is served in an unusual way. It is spread in a baking dish, topped with a cheese-accented cornmeal batter, and then baked. When done, the thin layer of cornbread is golden and light, and the rust-hued chili beneath is hot and spicy. A sprinkle of cilantro and a bowl of sour cream make fine finishing touches.

Serves 6

PREP TIME:
35 minutes, including
10 minutes for the
cornbread

START-TO-FINISH TIME:
2 hours, 10 minutes

MAKE AHEAD:
Yes, partially

Spicy Chili

3 tbsp olive or canola oil, plus more if needed

2 lb/910 g ground beef (85 percent lean works well)

2 cups/250 g chopped onion

1 tbsp minced garlic

¼ cup/30 g all-purpose flour

1½ tbsp chili powder

1½ tbsp ground cumin

1 tbsp dried oregano

1 to 1½ tsp chipotle chile powder (depending on how much heat you like)

Kosher salt

4 to 5½ cups/960 ml to 1.3 L reduced-sodium beef broth

One 28-oz/800-g can diced tomatoes, drained

Two 15½-oz/445-g cans black beans, rinsed and drained

1 large yellow bell pepper, stem, seeds, and membranes removed, and cut into ¼-in/6-mm dice

1. For the Spicy Chili: Heat the olive oil in a large, deep-sided pot (with a lid) over medium-high heat until hot. Add the ground beef and sauté, stirring often and breaking it up into small pieces with a wooden spoon, until browned, 6 to 8 minutes. Remove the beef with a slotted spoon and drain on paper towels. Pour off all but 2 tbsp of the drippings in the pan and return to medium-high heat. Add the onion and sauté, stirring, until softened and lightly browned, 4 to 5 minutes, using more oil if needed. Stir in the garlic and cook for 1 minute more. Return the beef to the pan.

2. Combine the flour, chili powder, cumin, oregano, chipotle chile powder, and 1 tsp salt in a small bowl. Sprinkle this mixture over the beef and onion, and cook, stirring, for 1 minute. Add 4 cups/960 ml of the beef broth and the tomatoes, and bring the mixture to a low boil. Cover the pan, lower the heat, and simmer for 5 minutes. Remove the lid and cook for 15 minutes more. If the liquid seems to be cooking down too quickly, add up to another 1½ cups/360 ml broth.

3. Add the black beans and yellow bell pepper to the chili. Raise the heat to high, and cook until the liquid has nearly evaporated, 15 to 20 minutes or more. Season with additional salt as needed. (The chili can be prepared up to this point 2 days ahead; cool, cover, and refrigerate. Reheat, uncovered, while stirring, over medium heat.)

continued . . .

4. Arrange a rack in the middle of the oven and preheat to 425°F/220°C. Spoon the chili into a 9-by-13-in/23-by-33-cm or another shallow 3-qt/2.8-L baking dish, and smooth out evenly with a rubber spatula.

5. For the Cornbread Crust: Mix together the cornmeal, flour, baking powder, salt, and baking soda in a medium bowl. In a large bowl, whisk together the buttermilk, egg, and canola oil. Gradually whisk the dry ingredients into the buttermilk mixture until blended. Stir in ½ cup/50 g of the cheddar and the 3 tbsp cilantro.

6. Pour the batter over the chili and spread evenly with a spatula (the batter will be thin). Sprinkle the remaining ½ cup/50 g cheese over the batter.

7. Bake the casserole until the cornbread topping is set and golden, 20 to 25 minutes. Remove from the oven and cool for 5 minutes. Garnish with the 2 tbsp cilantro and serve the chili with sour cream.

Cornbread Crust

¾ cup/105 g yellow cornmeal

½ cup/60 g all-purpose flour

1 tsp baking powder

1 tsp kosher salt

½ tsp baking soda

1 cup/240 ml buttermilk

1 large egg, lightly beaten

2 tbsp canola or vegetable oil

1 cup/100 g grated sharp white cheddar cheese

3 tbsp chopped fresh cilantro

2 tbsp chopped fresh cilantro

1 cup/225 ml sour cream for serving

Lamb and Spinach Phyllo Pie

Calliope Hoffman, a native of Crete, gave me tips on how to assemble this Greek-style dish and shared her special tomato and lamb sauce, which is used in the filling. This glorious savory pie, composed of layers of tomato-scented lamb and fresh spinach, is encased in buttered phyllo sheets, and then baked until the filling is hot and the pastry is golden and crisp.

Serves 6

PREP TIME:
45 minutes

START-TO-FINISH TIME:
2 hours

MAKE AHEAD:
No

4 tbsp/60 ml olive oil

2 lb/910 g ground lamb

2 cups/250 g chopped onion

2 tbsp chopped garlic

One 15-oz/430-g can tomato sauce

3 tbsp dried oregano

2 tsp dried thyme

Kosher salt

¼ tsp ground cinnamon

¾ cup/25 g chopped fresh flat-leaf parsley,
   plus 1 tbsp for garnish

1 large egg, beaten well

1 lb/455 g fresh baby spinach

½ cup/85 g creamy goat cheese,
   broken into pieces

1 tsp grated lemon zest

Seven 13-by-18-in/33-by-46-cm phyllo sheets,
   thawed in the refrigerator for 8 hours or
   overnight (see Market Note)

8 tbsp/115 g unsalted butter, melted

5 tbsp/40 g fine dry bread crumbs
   (see Market Note)

¾ cup/90 g grated Parmesan cheese,
   preferably Parmigiano-Reggiano

1. Arrange a rack in the lower third of the oven and preheat to 400°F/200°C. Generously butter a 9-by-13-in/23-by-33-cm baking dish.

2. Heat 2 tbsp of the olive oil in a large, heavy frying pan over medium heat. When hot, add the lamb, onion, and garlic. Cook, breaking up the meat with a wooden spoon and stirring often, until the lamb has browned and the onion is softened and translucent, about 5 minutes. Carefully spoon off any excess liquid in the frying pan.

3. Stir in the tomato sauce, oregano, thyme, ½ tsp salt, and the cinnamon. Cook, stirring often, for 4 minutes more. Mix in the ¾ cup/25 g parsley and season with more salt if needed. Set aside to cool for 10 minutes, and then stir in the beaten egg.

4. Heat the remaining 2 tbsp olive oil in a large, heavy frying pan over medium-low heat. When the oil is hot, add the spinach gradually, in large handfuls, and cook, stirring, until it has wilted. Continue to add the spinach in this way until all has wilted. Remove the pan from the heat and spoon off any excess liquid. Add the goat cheese and lemon zest, stirring until all the cheese has melted. Season with salt and set aside.

continued . . .

5. Cover a work surface with a clean kitchen towel. Place a phyllo sheet on the towel with the short end facing you. (Keep the remaining phyllo sheets covered with a lightly dampened kitchen towel, so they do not dry out.) Brush the sheet generously with some of the melted butter, and sprinkle with 1 tbsp of the bread crumbs. Repeat the process with five more sheets, stacking them one on top of the other, but omit the bread crumbs on the last sheet.

6. Transfer the stack of phyllo sheets to the prepared baking dish so that the phyllo extends evenly over the long sides of the dish. Spoon half of the lamb mixture evenly into the dish, and sprinkle ¼ cup/30 g of the Parmesan over it. Spread the spinach in an even layer over the lamb mixture, and sprinkle with ¼ cup/30 g Parmesan. Finally, spread the remaining lamb mixture over the spinach layer and sprinkle with the remaining ¼ cup/30 g Parmesan. Fold in the overhanging sides of the phyllo to cover the casserole and brush with butter. Brush the remaining phyllo sheet with butter and fold it in half lengthwise, buttered-side in, so that it will cover the top of the casserole. Place it in the baking dish and brush the top with butter.

7. Put the casserole in the preheated oven and reduce the temperature to 375°F/190°C. Bake until the top is golden brown, 25 to 30 minutes. Remove from the oven and cool for 10 minutes. Sprinkle with the remaining 1 tbsp chopped parsley before serving.

 MARKET NOTE:

Phyllo sheets come in various dimensions. Those that are 13 by 18 in/33 by 46 cm work perfectly in this recipe. Sometimes when you open a package of phyllo, you find that the leaves are torn or cracked. You can still use them; just brush them with plenty of butter, and layer them as directed—cracks, tears, and all.

Unseasoned store-bought bread crumbs, which tend to be very finely ground, work best in this recipe.

Deb Snow's Salmon and Corn Shepherd's Pies

My friend Deborah Snow, the talented chef at the Blue Heron in Sunderland, Massachusetts, believes in cooking seasonally. At the end of summer and into early fall, when local farms near her restaurant are spilling over with fresh corn and herbs, these individual shepherd's pies appear on her menu. She arranges sautéed salmon fillets and lightly caramelized corn kernels, scented with herbs, in baking dishes, and tops them with creamy whipped potatoes.

Serves 4

PREP TIME:
20 minutes

START-TO-FINISH TIME:
1 hour, 10 minutes

MAKE AHEAD:
Yes

Salmon and Corn Filling

4 salmon fillets (5 to 6 oz/140 to 170 g each, cut from the center section), about ¾ in/ 2 cm thick, skin removed (see Market Note, page 79)

1 tsp kosher salt

1 tsp freshly ground black pepper

4 tbsp/55 g unsalted butter

4 tbsp/60 ml canola oil

4 tsp fresh lemon juice

4 cups/600 g fresh corn kernels (6 to 7 ears)

1 cup/125 g chopped onion

Generous pinch of cayenne pepper

2 tbsp chopped fresh basil, plus 4 sprigs for garnish

1 tbsp plus 1 tsp chopped fresh flat-leaf parsley

1. Arrange a rack in the middle of the oven and preheat to 375°F/190°C. Generously butter four 5½-in/14-cm gratin or crème brûlée dishes and place them on a rimmed baking sheet.

2. For the Salmon and Corn Filling: Pat the salmon fillets dry with paper towels. Combine ½ tsp of the salt and ½ tsp of the black pepper in a small bowl and season the fish on both sides with this mixture. Melt 2 tbsp of the butter with 2 tbsp of the canola oil in a large, heavy frying pan over medium-high heat. When very hot, add the salmon fillets and sauté until barely starting to brown, 1 to 2 minutes per side. Place a fillet, skinned-side down, in each prepared gratin and, if necessary, tuck the slender part under so that it fits in the dish. Drizzle 1 tsp lemon juice over each fillet.

3. Discard any drippings in the frying pan and wipe it clean with paper towels. Return the pan to medium heat and add the remaining 2 tbsp butter and 2 tbsp oil. When hot, add the corn and onion and cook, stirring occasionally, until the corn is lightly browned and caramelized and the onion is translucent, 5 minutes or more. Season the corn with the remaining ½ tsp salt and ½ tsp black pepper and the cayenne pepper. Remove the pan from the heat and stir in the chopped basil and parsley. Divide the corn mixture evenly and spoon over and around the salmon fillets.

continued . . .

4. For the Whipped Potato Topping: Bring a large pot of water to a boil and add 1 tbsp salt. Cook the potatoes until tender, 15 minutes or more. Meanwhile, heat the half-and-half and butter in a small saucepan until warm and set aside.

5. When the potatoes are tender, drain them in a colander and return to the pot. With an electric hand mixer on medium speed, beat the potatoes until they are smooth. Gradually beat in the half-and-half mixture. Season the potatoes with ½ tsp salt and ¼ tsp black pepper, or more if needed. Divide the potatoes evenly among the gratins, mounding them on top. With a spatula, spread them in waves over the salmon and corn. (The casseroles can be prepared up to this point 45 minutes ahead; leave, uncovered, at cool room temperature.)

6. Bake the gratins until the potatoes are hot and the salmon is tender when pierced with a sharp knife, 10 to 12 minutes. (The baking time will vary, depending on how thick the fillets are.) Remove from the oven and garnish the center of each gratin with a basil sprig before serving.

Whipped Potato Topping

Kosher salt

1½ lb/680 g Yukon gold potatoes, peeled and cut into 1-in/2.5-cm cubes

1 cup/240 ml half-and-half

3 tbsp unsalted butter

Freshly ground black pepper

Shrimp, Tomatoes, and Artichokes Under Saffron Croutons

This casserole looks as if it takes far more effort to make than required. In fact, it is simplicity itself. You add shrimp to a quickly prepared tomato and artichoke sauce, and spoon the mixture into a baking dish. A sprinkle of crumbled feta and a topping of homemade croutons complete the assembly before the dish goes in the oven for a few minutes of baking.

Serves 6

PREP TIME:
30 minutes

START-TO-FINISH TIME:
1 hour, 10 minutes

MAKE AHEAD:
No

1 day-old baguette

2 tbsp olive oil, plus ¼ cup/60 ml

¼ tsp saffron threads, crushed

½ cup/65 g chopped onion

One 9-oz/255-g package frozen artichoke
  hearts, defrosted and patted dry

2 tbsp all-purpose flour

1 tbsp chopped garlic

1 tsp dried basil

1 tsp dried oregano

⅛ tsp red pepper flakes

One 28-oz/800-g can diced tomatoes,
  with their juices

¼ cup/60 ml white wine

½ cup/75 g pitted Kalamata olives, quartered
  lengthwise

Kosher salt

1 lb/455 g extra-large (16 to 20 count) shrimp,
  shelled and deveined

½ cup/80 g crumbled feta cheese

2 tbsp chopped fresh basil

1. Arrange a rack in the middle of the oven and preheat to 50°F/180°C. Oil a 9-by-13-in/23-by-33-cm or another shallow 3-qt/2.8-L baking dish.

2. Cut the baguette into ¾-in/2-cm slices, and cut the slices into ¾-in/2-cm cubes to get 2 cups/85 g. (Save the extra bread for another use.) Mix the 2 tbsp olive oil and the saffron in a medium bowl, add the bread cubes, and toss to coat well. Spread the bread on a rimmed baking sheet and bake until golden and crisp, turning once, 7 to 8 minutes. Remove from the oven and set aside.

3. Heat the ¼ cup/60 ml olive oil in a large, heavy frying pan over medium heat until hot. Add the onion and artichoke hearts and sauté, stirring often, until the onion is slightly translucent, 3 to 5 minutes. Add the flour, garlic, basil, oregano, and red pepper flakes and cook, stirring, for 1½ minutes. Add the tomatoes and their juices, the wine, and olives and stir to combine. Season with ½ tsp salt, adding more if needed.

4. Remove the pan from the heat and stir in the shrimp. Spoon the mixture into the prepared baking dish. Sprinkle with the feta and top with the croutons. Bake, uncovered, until the shrimp are pink and curled, about 12 minutes. (The cooking time may vary, depending on the size of the shrimp; larger ones will take more time.)

5. Sprinkle the casserole with the chopped basil before serving.

CASSEROLES WITH PASTA

Sauced, Stuffed, and Layered

If asked to choose the ingredient that inspires the most creative casseroles, it wouldn't take me long to declare pasta the winner. Available in all shapes and sizes, in fresh or dried varieties, pasta is a canvas waiting for a cook's artistic expression.

The following recipes reflect the bounty of pasta choices, including rigatoni, farfalle, and elbow macaroni, which are interchangeable, as well as large pasta shells for stuffing. Strands of fettuccine and pappardelle (also interchangeable) are the foundations of other casseroles. Whichever one you choose, cook the pasta in a large amount of water to prevent it from sticking together, and add plenty of salt for flavor.

Busy cooks who don't want to bother with making white sauces (used so often to bind baked pasta dishes) will love Farfalle with Asparagus, Roasted Shallots, and Creamy Blue Cheese (page 141). In place of a béchamel, a generous amount of Gorgonzola is combined with the warm pasta and other ingredients, melting to form a luscious sauce. The same time-saving technique works for Pappardelle with Cauliflower, Leeks, and Mushrooms (page 136), in which mascarpone and Parmesan melt effortlessly together into a sauce.

The casseroles in this chapter play varied roles and fill different needs. Some have become trusted standbys when I entertain, while others grace my kitchen table for family meals. Both Rigatoni with Spicy Tomato Sauce, Kalamatas, and Two Cheeses (page 139) and Wild Mushroom Lasagna (page 145) are make-ahead dishes, perfect for serving a crowd. For weeknight menus, turn to Caraway Noodle Casserole with Black Forest Ham, Carrots, and Peas (page 152). Most of these pasta creations are meant to anchor a menu, but Crab-Stuffed Pasta Shells with Orange-Scented Tomato Sauce (page 150) makes a striking first course, and, of course, classic Mac and Cheese (page 134) is everyone's favorite side.

Mac and Cheese—the Classic and Variations

There are probably as many versions of macaroni and cheese as there are cooks. My friends, my cooking students, and my colleagues all profess to have the definitive recipe for this American favorite. This version is one I created over a long period of time. It calls for covering the pasta very generously with cheese sauce, so that it does not dry out during baking. A topping of golden, crusty homemade bread crumbs contrasts with the creamy pasta beneath. One final addition distinguishes this mac and cheese from others: Crème fraîche is included in the cheese sauce, providing a refreshing tartness to balance the richness of this dish. And if you want a change from the classic, try one of the three interesting variations that follow this recipe.

Serves 4 as a main course, or 5 or 6 as a side dish

PREP TIME:
15 minutes

START-TO-FINISH TIME:
1 hour, 15 minutes

MAKE AHEAD:
Yes, partially

8 oz/225 g elbow macaroni

Kosher salt

2 tbsp unsalted butter

2 tbsp all-purpose flour

1 cup/240 ml whole milk

1 cup/240 ml crème fraîche, homemade (see page 12) or store-bought

2½ cups/250 g grated extra-sharp white cheddar cheese

¼ cup/15 g Toasted Bread Crumbs (page 12)

1. Arrange a rack in the middle of the oven and preheat to 350°F/180°C. Generously butter a 2-qt/2-L baking dish.

2. Bring a large pot of water to a boil, and add the macaroni and 1 tbsp salt. Cook according to the package directions, drain well, and transfer to a large mixing bowl.

3. Melt the butter in a medium saucepan over medium heat. When hot, add the flour and cook, stirring constantly, for 1½ to 2 minutes. Gradually pour in the milk and spoon in the crème fraîche, whisking constantly until the mixture comes to a gentle boil, 3 to 4 minutes. Remove from the heat and stir in 2¼ cups/225 g of the cheddar cheese, a handful at a time (the mixture will be soupy). Season the sauce with ¾ tsp salt.

4. Pour the sauce into the bowl with the macaroni and stir well to combine. Spread evenly in the prepared baking dish. (The casserole can be made up to this point 1 day ahead; cool, cover, and refrigerate. Bring to room temperature 30 minutes before baking.)

5. Sprinkle the bread crumbs over the macaroni, followed by the remaining ¼ cup/25 g cheddar cheese. Bake the macaroni until the top is golden and bubbling, 25 to 30 minutes. Remove from the oven and let sit for 10 minutes before serving.

VARIATIONS:

MAC AND LOBSTER WITH LEMON AND TARRAGON

Combine the macaroni and sauce in the bowl. Cut 6 oz/170 g cooked lobster into 1-in/2.5-cm pieces, and stir into the macaroni. Add 1 tbsp plus 1 tsp grated lemon zest and 1 tbsp plus 1 tsp chopped fresh tarragon. Pour the mixture into the baking dish, top with bread crumbs and cheese, and bake as directed.

MAC WITH PEAS AND PANCETTA

Combine the macaroni and sauce in the bowl. Sauté 4 oz/115 g finely diced pancetta until light golden and crisp, about 3 to 4 minutes. Drain on paper towels and stir into the macaroni. Add ½ cup/75 g peas (if fresh, blanch for 2 minutes; if frozen, defrost), and ⅓ cup/30 g chopped green onion. Pour the mixture into the baking dish, top with bread crumbs and cheese, and bake as directed.

MAC WITH SMOKED SAUSAGE AND COUNTRY MUSTARD

Combine the macaroni and sauce in the bowl. Cut a 4-oz/115-g piece of kielbasa in half lengthwise, and slice ⅛ in/3 mm thick. Sauté over medium heat until lightly browned, 3 to 4 minutes; drain on paper towels. Add the sausage along with 1½ tsp coarse-grain Dijon mustard to the macaroni. Pour the mixture into the baking dish, top with bread crumbs and cheese, and bake as directed.

Pappardelle with Cauliflower, Leeks, and Mushrooms

Nothing is a bigger thrill for me when I'm in Paris, even when it's freezing outside, than to go to the city's popular Marché Bio. Even my spouse, an avowed noncook, admits that this food market, featuring organic products, is fascinating. One especially cold Sunday, our haul included a bag of fresh shiitake mushrooms, a bunch of leeks, and a beautiful head of cauliflower, all of which I used to make this simple yet satisfying vegetarian casserole. This dish takes only about 1 hour from start to finish and can be prepared several hours ahead.

Serves 4 to 6

PREP TIME:
25 minutes

START-TO-FINISH TIME:
1 hour

MAKE AHEAD:
Yes

10 oz/280 g shiitake mushrooms

1 head cauliflower

6 tbsp/85 g unsalted butter

3 tbsp olive oil

2½ cups/240 g chopped leeks (white and light green parts only, 3 to 4 leeks)

Kosher salt

12 oz/340 g pappardelle pasta (see Market Note)

1 cup/240 ml mascarpone

¾ cup/90 g grated Parmesan cheese, preferably Parmigiano-Reggiano

Freshly ground black pepper

1 tbsp chopped fresh flat-leaf parsley (optional)

1. Arrange a rack in the middle of the oven and preheat to 375°F/190°C. Generously butter a 9-by-13-in/23-by-33-cm or another shallow 3-qt/2.8-L baking dish.

2. Remove the stems from the mushrooms and discard or save for another use. Wipe the caps clean with a dampened paper towel and cut them into ½-in-/12-mm-wide strips.

3. Remove the base from the cauliflower and cut the head into florets. Cut the florets into ¼-in-/6-mm-thick slices to yield 3 cups/280 g. (Save any extra for another use.)

4. Melt 3 tbsp of the butter with the olive oil in a large, heavy frying pan over medium heat. When hot, add the mushrooms and leeks. Cook, stirring often, until both are softened and lightly browned, 5 to 7 minutes. Remove the frying pan from the heat and set aside.

5. Bring a large pot of water to a boil. Add the cauliflower slices and 1 tbsp salt and cook until tender when pierced with a sharp knife, 4 to 5 minutes. Remove with a slotted spoon to drain. Add the pappardelle to the pot and cook according to the package directions. Drain well in a colander and return the pasta to the empty pot. Add the remaining 3 tbsp butter, the mascarpone, and ½ cup/60 g of the Parmesan, stirring until all have melted. Add the mushroom and leek mixture and the cauliflower; toss to mix. Season the mixture with ¾ tsp salt and ¼ tsp black pepper, or more if needed.

6. Spoon the pasta and vegetables into the prepared baking dish and sprinkle the remaining ¼ cup/30 g Parmesan cheese over the top. Cover the casserole tightly with foil. (The casserole can be prepared up to this point 6 hours ahead; cool, cover, and refrigerate. Bring to room temperature 30 minutes before continuing.)

7. Bake the casserole, covered, until it is hot and the cheese on top has melted, 15 to 20 minutes.

8. Remove from the oven and garnish with parsley, if desired, before serving.

 MARKET NOTE:

If pappardelle (wide pasta strands) is unavailable, substitute fettuccine.

Rigatoni with Spicy Tomato Sauce, Kalamatas, and Two Cheeses

This is my "go-to" casserole for potlucks, for suppers for my husband's college students, and for weekend company guests. It can be completely assembled in advance, serves a crowd, and has bold, striking flavors. The name says it all—tube-shaped pasta are coated in a tomato sauce with an extra kick of heat from red pepper flakes, while creamy Havarti and Parmesan cheese add a luscious smoothness, and slivered olives provide a salty accent.

Serves 6

PREP TIME:
30 minutes

START-TO-FINISH TIME:
1 hour, 50 minutes

MAKE AHEAD:
Yes

FREEZE:
Yes, before baking (see directions on page 11)

6 tbsp/90 ml olive oil

1½ cups/190 g chopped onion

1 tsp finely chopped garlic

Three 28-oz/800-g cans diced tomatoes, drained

2 tsp dried basil

Scant 1½ tsp red pepper flakes, plus more if needed

Kosher salt

¼ tsp freshly ground black pepper

2 cups/480 ml reduced-sodium chicken broth (see Cooking Tip)

1 lb/455 g rigatoni, large macaroni, or penne pasta

2½ cups/290 g shredded Havarti cheese

⅓ cup/40 g freshly grated Parmesan cheese, preferably Parmigiano-Reggiano

⅓ cup/50 g pitted and halved Kalamata olives

¼ cup/10 g finely chopped fresh basil or flat-leaf parsley

1. Arrange a rack in the middle of the oven and preheat to 350°F/180°C. Lightly oil a 9-by-13-in/23-by-33-cm or another shallow 3-qt/2.8-L baking dish.

2. Heat 3 tbsp of the olive oil in a large, heavy frying pan over medium-high heat. When the oil is hot, add the onion and garlic and sauté, stirring, for 3 minutes. Add the tomatoes, dried basil, red pepper flakes, 1 tsp salt, and the black pepper and stir well. Add the chicken broth and bring to a low boil.

3. Cook until the liquid has reduced and the mixture is chunky, 25 to 30 minutes. Remove from the heat, taste, and season with more salt and red pepper flakes, if desired. (The sauce can be made 1 day ahead; cool, cover, and refrigerate. Reheat before using.)

4. Bring a large pot of water to a boil and add the rigatoni and 1 tbsp salt. Cook according to the package directions. Drain well in a colander. Transfer the pasta to the prepared baking dish and toss with the remaining 3 tbsp oil; season with more salt if needed. Add the warm tomato sauce to the pasta and toss well to combine. Add the Havarti and toss again. Sprinkle the Parmesan over the top. Arrange the olives over the pasta. (The casserole can be prepared up to this point 1 day ahead. Cool, cover, and refrigerate. Bring to room temperature 30 minutes before baking.)

continued . . .

5. Bake the casserole, uncovered, until hot and bubbly, 25 to 30 minutes. Remove from the oven and sprinkle with the fresh basil before serving.

COOKING TIP:

If you want to make this dish strictly vegetarian, substitute a good vegetable broth for the chicken broth.

Farfalle with Asparagus, Roasted Shallots, and Creamy Blue Cheese

When you want a vegetarian dish with bright, assertive flavors, this casserole is the answer. The main ingredients shine individually, but the whole is greater than its parts. The sweetness of the roasted shallots, the saltiness of the cheese, and the distinctive taste of fresh asparagus work well together when combined with farfalle (the Italian word for "butterflies"), or bow-tie pasta. This casserole can be assembled several hours ahead, ready to pop in the oven at serving time.

Serves 6

PREP TIME:
25 minutes

START-TO-FINISH TIME:
1 hour, 30 minutes

MAKE AHEAD:
Yes

1½ lb/680 g shallots (about 24 medium), peeled and halved lengthwise, or quartered if large
2 tbsp olive oil
Kosher salt
Freshly ground black pepper
1 lb/455 g farfalle pasta
2 lb/910 g thin asparagus, trimmed and cut diagonally into 1½-in/4-cm pieces
12 oz/340 g creamy blue cheese, such as Gorgonzola or Gorgonzola dolce, rind removed and cut into ½-in/12-mm cubes
1 cup/55 g Toasted Bread Crumbs (page 12)

1. Arrange a rack in the middle of the oven and preheat to 375°F/190°C. Generously butter a 9-by-13-in/23-by-33-cm or another shallow 3-qt/2.8-L baking dish.

2. Put the shallots on a rimmed baking sheet, drizzle with the olive oil, and toss well to coat. Sprinkle with salt and pepper. Roast until the shallots are golden brown and very tender, stirring occasionally, 30 to 35 minutes. Remove from the oven and set aside at room temperature. Leave the oven on.

3. Bring a large pot of water to a boil and add the farfalle and 1 tbsp salt. Cook according to the package directions. During the last 4 minutes of cooking, add the asparagus to the pot and cook until crisp-tender. Drain the pasta and asparagus in a large colander and transfer to a large bowl. Add the Gorgonzola and toss. Add the roasted shallots to the bowl and toss again to combine. Season with salt and pepper.

4. Spread the pasta mixture evenly in the prepared baking dish. (The casserole can be prepared up to this point 6 hours ahead. Cool, cover, and refrigerate. Bring to room temperature 30 minutes before baking.)

5. Sprinkle with the bread crumbs and bake until the casserole is hot, 15 to 20 minutes. Serve immediately.

Pasta Spirals with Ricotta and Prosciutto

During a long stay in France one spring, I went often to La Grande Epicerie, the celebrated food emporium housed in Paris's Bon Marché department store. Each time I passed the counter of takeout dishes, I was intrigued by a display of lasagna spirals, composed of single sheets of pasta wrapped around interesting fillings. Back home, I created my own version: I spread a simple mix of ricotta, Parmesan, prosciutto, and Italian parsley on individual cooked lasagna noodles, rolled them up, and napped them with a zesty tomato sauce. This delectable main course is perfect for entertaining, since you can assemble the dish completely in advance, pop it in the fridge, and have it ready and waiting to be baked in about half an hour.

Serves 4

PREP TIME:
20 minutes

START-TO-FINISH TIME:
2 hours

MAKE AHEAD:
Yes

Zesty Tomato Sauce
2 tbsp olive oil
1 cup/125 g finely chopped onion
⅓ cup/50 g finely chopped carrot
2 tsp chopped garlic
1 tsp dried oregano
1 tsp dried basil
Kosher salt
¼ tsp red pepper flakes
One 28-oz/800-g can diced tomatoes, drained
2 cups/480 ml reduced-sodium chicken broth
⅓ cup/75 ml red wine

1. Arrange a rack in the middle of the oven and preheat to 375°F/190°C. Oil a 9-by-13-in/23-by-33-cm or another shallow 3-qt/2.8-L baking dish.

2. For the Zesty Tomato Sauce: Heat the olive oil in a large, heavy frying pan over medium-high heat until hot. Add the onion and carrot, and sauté, stirring, until softened, 3 to 4 minutes. Add the garlic and sauté for 1 minute more. Stir in the oregano, basil, ½ tsp salt, and the red pepper flakes. Add the tomatoes, chicken broth, and wine; stir well to blend. Cook, stirring occasionally, until the liquid has reduced by half, about 15 minutes. Purée the sauce in a food processor or blender or with a food mill. Taste and season with more salt if needed.

3. For the Pasta Spirals: Bring a large pot of water to a boil. Add the salt and lasagna noodles. Cook according to the package directions. Drain the noodles well in a colander and place on a damp kitchen towel; cover with another damp kitchen towel.

continued . . .

4. Mix together the prosciutto, ricotta, 1⅓ cups/155 g of the Parmesan, the parsley, and several grinds of pepper in a mixing bowl. Place a lasagna noodle on a cutting board, and spread a generous ⅓ cup/50 g of the filling on it, leaving a ¼-in/6-mm border on all sides. Cut the noodle in half crosswise. Starting at a short end, roll each half into a cylinder. Repeat with the remaining lasagna noodles. You will have sixteen pasta spirals.

5. Spread half of the sauce on the bottom of the prepared baking dish. Arrange the pasta spirals, seam-side down, in the dish. Brush them lightly with the olive oil, and then nap the centers with the remaining sauce and sprinkle with the remaining ⅓ cup/35 g Parmesan cheese. Cover the dish tightly with foil. (The pasta spirals can be prepared up to this point 1 day ahead and refrigerated. Bring to room temperature 30 minutes before baking.)

6. Bake the spirals, covered, until they are hot and the cheese on top has melted, 30 to 35 minutes. Remove the foil and sprinkle the remaining 2 tbsp parsley over the spirals before serving.

Pasta Spirals

1 tbsp kosher salt

8 dried lasagna noodles (see Market Note)

6 oz/180 g thinly sliced prosciutto, coarsely chopped

2 cups/455 g ricotta cheese

1⅔ cups/190 g grated Parmesan cheese, preferably Parmigiano-Reggiano

⅓ cup/15 g chopped fresh flat-leaf parsley

Freshly ground black pepper

2 tbsp olive oil

2 tbsp chopped fresh flat-leaf parsley

 MARKET NOTE:

Standard dried lasagna noodles are about 2 in/ 5 cm by 10 in/25 cm, which is the right size for this recipe.

Wild Mushroom Lasagna

"Celestial" is how I'd describe this special-occasion lasagna, which can be assembled completely a day ahead. Layers of noodles are spread with a delectable porcini mushroom and tomato sauce and also with a creamy béchamel. Plenty of rosemary and Parmigiano-Reggiano cheese round out the flavors.

Serves 6

PREP TIME:
35 minutes

START-TO-FINISH TIME:
2 hours, 40 minutes

MAKE AHEAD:
Yes

FREEZE:
Yes, before baking
(see directions on
page 11)

Mushroom Sauce

1½ oz/40 g dried porcini mushrooms

2 cups/480 ml boiling water

3 tbsp olive oil

1 cup/125 g chopped onion

1 lb/455 g white or brown mushrooms
(cremini), cleaned, ends trimmed, and
thinly sliced

1 tbsp chopped garlic

1 tbsp crushed dried rosemary (see Market
Note, page 34)

Kosher salt

Freshly ground black pepper

⅔ cup/165 ml dry white wine

One 28-oz/800-g can diced tomatoes,
drained well

1. Arrange a rack in the middle of the oven and preheat to 350°F/180°C. Butter a 9-by-13-in/23-by-33-cm baking dish.

2. For the Mushroom Sauce: Put the porcini mushrooms in a strainer and rinse under running water to remove any grit. Place them in a small bowl and soak in the boiling water for 20 minutes. Strain the mushrooms and soaking liquid over a bowl through a strainer lined with a paper towel, pressing down on the mushrooms with a spoon to extract as much liquid as possible. Reserve the soaking liquid. Coarsely chop the mushrooms.

3. Heat the olive oil in a large, heavy frying pan over medium-high heat. When hot, add the onion and sauté, stirring, until golden, about 4 minutes. Add the sliced mushrooms and sauté, stirring, until lightly browned and their liquid has evaporated, 10 to 12 minutes. Add the porcini, garlic, and dried rosemary and cook for 2 minutes more. Season with 1½ tsp salt and ¼ tsp pepper.

4. Add the strained porcini soaking liquid and the wine to the frying pan, and cook until the liquid has almost evaporated, 12 to 15 minutes, scraping any browned particles on the bottom of the pan into the mixture. Lower the heat to medium, add the tomatoes, and cook, stirring often, until any liquids have evaporated, 6 to 8 minutes. Taste and season with more salt and pepper if needed. Remove from the heat and set aside.

continued . . .

5. For the White Sauce with Nutmeg: Melt the butter in a large saucepan over medium heat. Add the flour and cook, stirring constantly, for 1½ to 2 minutes. Add the milk and bring to a gentle boil, whisking constantly until the mixture thickens enough to coat the back of a spoon, 4 to 5 minutes. Season the sauce with the salt, several grinds of pepper, and the nutmeg; set aside.

6. Bring a large pot of water to a boil and add 1 tbsp salt and the lasagna noodles. Cook according to the package directions. Drain the noodles well in a colander and place them on a damp kitchen towel; cover with another damp kitchen towel.

7. Arrange one-third of the noodles lengthwise in the prepared baking dish, just slightly overlapping. Spread one-fourth of the white sauce over the pasta, and, with a spatula (an offset one works well), spread one-third of the mushroom sauce on top. Sprinkle with ⅓ cup/40 g of the Parmesan cheese. Repeat the layers two more times. Spread the remaining white sauce over the pasta, sprinkle with the remaining ½ cup/60 g Parmesan, and dot with the butter. (The lasagna can be prepared up to this point 1 day ahead; cover with plastic wrap and refrigerate. Bring to room temperature 30 minutes before baking.)

8. Bake the lasagna, uncovered, until it is hot and the top is golden, 30 to 40 minutes. Remove from the oven and cool for 10 minutes. Cut into six portions and garnish each one, if desired, with a rosemary sprig before serving.

White Sauce with Nutmeg

6 tbsp/85 g unsalted butter

4½ tbsp/45 g all-purpose flour

3 cups/720 ml whole milk

½ tsp kosher salt

Freshly ground black pepper

¼ tsp freshly grated nutmeg

1 tbsp kosher salt

9 dried lasagna noodles (9 oz/255 g total;
  see Cooking Tip)

1½ cups/180 g grated Parmesan cheese,
  preferably Parmigiano-Reggiano

2 tbsp unsalted butter

6 fresh rosemary sprigs for garnish (optional)

COOKING TIP:

"No-boil" dried lasagna noodles do not work well in this recipe.

Fettuccine with Chicken, Fennel, and Lemon Cream

In my cooking classes, every time I anchor a menu with this casserole, students respond the same way: They savor the delectable mélange of flavors and love the easy preparation. Cooked fettuccine noodles along with poached chicken breasts, fennel, and prosciutto are coated with a silky smooth lemon cream sauce, and then sprinkled with Gruyère and baked.

Serves 6

PREP TIME:
25 minutes

START-TO-FINISH TIME:
1 hour, 30 minutes

MAKE AHEAD:
Yes

FREEZE:
Yes, before baking
(see directions on
page 11)

1 large or 2 medium fennel bulbs and greens

4 cups/960 ml reduced-sodium chicken broth

6 boneless, skinless chicken breast halves
    (about 6 oz/170 g each; see Market Note)

2 tbsp unsalted butter

2 tbsp all-purpose flour

1 cup/240 ml heavy or whipping cream

3 tbsp fresh lemon juice

1 tsp fennel seeds, crushed (see page 12)

1½ cups/120 g shredded Gruyère cheese

Kosher salt

8 to 9 oz/225 to 255 g fresh fettuccine pasta

4 oz/115 g thinly sliced prosciutto,
    cut into strips about 3 in/7.5 long
    and ¼ in/6 mm wide

Freshly ground black pepper

1. Arrange a rack in the middle of the oven and preheat to 350°F/180°C. Generously butter a 9-by-13-in/23-by-33-cm or another shallow 3-qt/2.8-L baking dish.

2. Trim the stalks from the fennel, reserving several of the lacy sprigs for garnish. Halve the bulbs lengthwise and cut out the tough cores. Slice the fennel lengthwise into ¼-in/6-mm strips.

3. Bring the chicken broth to a simmer in a large saucepan over medium-high heat. Add the fennel and cook until just tender, 8 to 10 minutes. Remove with a slotted spoon and set aside. Add the chicken breasts and simmer until cooked through, 8 to 10 minutes. Remove the chicken to a cutting board (save the cooking liquid). When the chicken is cool enough to handle, hold a knife parallel to the work surface and slice each breast in half through the center. (If the chicken has not cooked thoroughly, put the breasts back into the broth and cook for another minute or two.) Set aside the chicken and the cooking liquid.

4. Melt the butter in a medium saucepan over medium heat. Add the flour and cook, stirring constantly, for 1½ to 2 minutes. Gradually whisk in the cream and 1 cup/240 ml of the reserved cooking liquid (discard the rest or save for another use). Bring to a gentle boil, whisking constantly until the mixture thickens enough to coat the back of a spoon, 4 to 5 minutes. Stir in the lemon juice, fennel seeds, and half of the Gruyère and mix well. Season with salt if needed.

5. Bring a large pot of water to a boil. Add 1 tbsp salt and the fettuccine. Cook according to the package directions. Drain well in a colander, and spread in the prepared dish. Toss the pasta with half of the sauce. Add half of the fennel and half of the prosciutto, and toss again to combine.

6. Arrange the chicken breasts on top in a single layer and season generously with salt and pepper. Pour the remaining sauce over the chicken, and then scatter the remaining fennel and prosciutto on top. Sprinkle with the remaining Gruyère. (The casserole can be prepared up to this point 1 day ahead; cool, cover, and refrigerate. Bring to room temperature 30 minutes before baking.)

7. Bake, uncovered, until the cheese has melted and the chicken is hot, about 20 minutes. Cool for 5 to 10 minutes. Garnish the center of the dish with several of the reserved fennel sprigs. For serving, use a sharp knife if necessary (to cut though the chicken breasts on the top layer).

MARKET NOTE:

Chicken breasts often run large in today's markets; try to find smaller ones for this recipe so that they will fit snugly in a single layer in the casserole.

Crab-Stuffed Pasta Shells with Orange-Scented Tomato Sauce

Tomatoes and orange, two distinctive flavors with a natural affinity for each other, are particularly good when combined with shellfish like crab. In this casserole, a tomato sauce with robust accents of orange zest and fresh basil is the perfect foil for large pasta shells mounded with a light crab and bread crumb filling. You can prepare the sauce a couple of days ahead and stuff the shells a few hours in advance, so only a quick assembly will be required before you bake and serve the dish.

Serves 4

PREP TIME:
30 minutes

START-TO-FINISH TIME:
2 hours

MAKE AHEAD:
Yes, partially

Orange-Scented Tomato Sauce

2 tbsp olive oil

¾ cup/95 g chopped onion

⅓ cup/45 g chopped carrot

1 tbsp chopped fresh basil (see Market Note)

1 tsp chopped garlic

Kosher salt

Scant ⅛ tsp red pepper flakes

One 28-oz/800-g can diced tomatoes, drained well

1½ cups/360 ml reduced-sodium chicken broth

2 tsp grated orange zest

Generous pinch of sugar, plus more if needed

1. Arrange a rack in the middle of the oven and preheat to 375°F/190°C. Generously oil a 9-by-13-in/23-by-33-cm or another shallow 3-qt/2.8-L baking dish.

2. For the Orange-Scented Tomato Sauce: Heat the olive oil in a large, heavy frying pan (with a lid) over medium heat. When hot, add the onion and carrot and cook, stirring, until the vegetables are slightly softened, 3 to 4 minutes. Add the basil, garlic, ¼ tsp salt, and the red pepper flakes and cook, stirring, for 2 minutes more. Stir in the tomatoes, chicken broth, orange zest, and sugar.

3. Bring the mixture to a simmer, reduce the heat, and cover. Simmer until the vegetables are tender, about 20 minutes. Season the sauce with more salt and even an additional pinch of sugar if needed. Purée the sauce in a food processor or blender or with a food mill, and return to the pan. You should have about 3 cups/720 ml. (The sauce can be prepared 2 days ahead; cool, cover, and refrigerate. Reheat over medium heat.)

4. Bring a large pot of water to a boil and add 1 tbsp salt and the pasta shells. Cook until quite tender, 15 to 20 minutes. (These shells often take longer than the package directions suggest.) Drain in a colander, and pat dry with a clean kitchen towel.

5. In a medium frying pan over medium heat, melt 4 tbsp/55 g of the butter until hot. Add the green onions and celery and cook, stirring, until just tender, 4 to 5 minutes. Add the bread crumbs and stir for 1 minute more to moisten. Remove the frying pan from the heat and stir in half of the basil, the lemon juice, lemon zest, and orange zest. Mix well and blend in the crabmeat, ½ tsp salt, and the eggs. Fill the shells with the crab mixture. (The shells can be prepared up to this point 6 hours ahead; cover and refrigerate.)

6. Melt the remaining 1 tbsp butter. Ladle half of the sauce on the bottom of the prepared baking dish. Place the shells in the dish and brush them lightly with the melted butter to keep them from drying out. Nap the center of each pasta shell with some of the remaining sauce.

7. Bake, uncovered, until the shells are hot, 30 to 35 minutes, or longer if they have been refrigerated. Remove from the oven and sprinkle with the remaining basil before serving.

Kosher salt

16 large pasta shells (2 to 2½ in/5 to 6 cm)

5 tbsp/70 g unsalted butter

1 cup/90 g chopped green onions (including 2 in/5 cm of the green stems)

⅓ cup/40 g chopped celery

2½ cups/140 g fresh bread crumbs, preferably made from sourdough bread

¼ cup plus 2 tbsp/15 g chopped fresh basil

1 tbsp plus 1 tsp fresh lemon juice, plus 1 tsp grated lemon zest

1½ tsp grated orange zest

8 oz/225 g fresh crabmeat

2 large eggs, beaten well

 MARKET NOTE:

A bunch of fresh basil will go a long way in this recipe. A hint of this fresh herb gives the sauce a sophisticated taste, and you'll need more for the pasta stuffing and the garnish.

Caraway Noodle Casserole with Black Forest Ham, Carrots, and Peas

This is an old-fashioned casserole, with ham and noodles baked in a creamy sauce, but it has been updated with a hint of caraway. The crushed seeds add extra flavor to the sauce, and are echoed in the toasted bread crumb topping, prepared with caraway-scented rye. Like most pasta casseroles, this one can be completely assembled ahead of time and baked when needed.

Serves 4

PREP TIME:
20 minutes

START-TO-FINISH TIME:
1 hour, 15 minutes

MAKE AHEAD:
Yes

Caraway Cheese Sauce

2 tbsp unsalted butter

2 tbsp all-purpose flour

2 cups/480 ml whole milk

1 tsp caraway seeds, toasted and crushed (see page 12)

Kosher salt

½ tsp freshly ground black pepper

¾ cup/60 g grated Gruyère cheese

1 tbsp kosher salt

8 oz/225 g extra-wide egg noodles

1 tbsp unsalted butter

8 oz/225 g Black Forest ham, cut into ¼-in/ 6-mm dice (see Market Note)

½ cup/70 g finely diced carrot (¼-in/6-mm dice)

¾ cup/60 g chopped leeks (white and light green parts only)

½ cup/75 g shelled fresh peas or frozen peas, defrosted

¾ cup/60 g grated Gruyère cheese

½ cup/30 g Toasted Bread Crumbs (page 12) made from rye bread with caraway seeds, toasted in butter

1. Arrange a rack in the middle of the oven and preheat to 350°F/180°C. Generously butter a 2- to 2½-qt/2- to 2.4-L shallow baking dish.

2. For the Caraway Cheese Sauce: Melt the butter in a medium saucepan over medium heat. Add the flour and cook, stirring constantly, for 1½ to 2 minutes. Gradually pour in the milk, whisking constantly until the mixture is smooth and starts to simmer. Whisk in the caraway seeds, 1 tsp salt, and the pepper, and then gradually whisk in the Gruyère. Season with more salt if needed and set aside.

3. Bring a large pot of water to a boil and add 1 tbsp salt and the noodles. Cook according to the package directions. Drain well in a colander, and transfer to a large mixing bowl.

4. Melt the butter in a large, heavy frying pan over medium heat. When hot, add the ham and carrot. Sauté, stirring often, until the ham is lightly browned and the carrot is just tender, about 5 minutes. Stir in the leeks and peas and sauté, stirring frequently, until the leeks become translucent, about 2 minutes. Add the ham and vegetables to the bowl with the noodles and stir in the sauce. Mix well to combine and spread evenly in the prepared baking dish.

Sprinkle the Gruyère over the top. (The casserole can be prepared up to this point 2 hours ahead; cool, cover, and refrigerate. Bring to room temperature for 30 minutes before baking.)

5. Sprinkle the bread crumbs over the casserole. Bake, uncovered, until the cheese has melted, 20 to 25 minutes. Serve immediately.

 MARKET NOTE:

Black Forest ham is a well-seasoned smoked ham, which is available in the deli section of most supermarkets. In Europe, ham labeled as Black Forest must come from the Black Forest region of Germany, but in the United States, hams prepared in the Black Forest style are sold under this name.

BREAKFAST CASSEROLES

Big and Small, Morning Wake-Up Calls

Casseroles aren't just for lunch and dinner. You can start your day with a special baked dish as well. What could be better to serve family and friends for breakfast or brunch than a savory or sweet casserole taken piping hot from the oven? An added advantage is that many of these dishes can be assembled in advance, and then baked when needed.

Most of the recipes in this chapter feature eggs. You can choose from a Spanish tortilla prepared with potatoes and chorizo or an Italian frittata with caramelized onions and herbs. Both are baked, rather than cooked on the stove top. Two glorious casseroles—Emily's Souffléd Eggs with Cheddar and Green Chiles (page 158) and the Mushroom Popover Casserole (page 161)—have ethereally light textures, and would be showstoppers for any morning meal.

Round out your menu with a mixed green salad and a dessert of seasonal fruits—berries in the spring, melon wedges in the summer, perfectly ripe pears and apples in the fall, and grapefruit and orange segments in the winter. Breakfast is served!

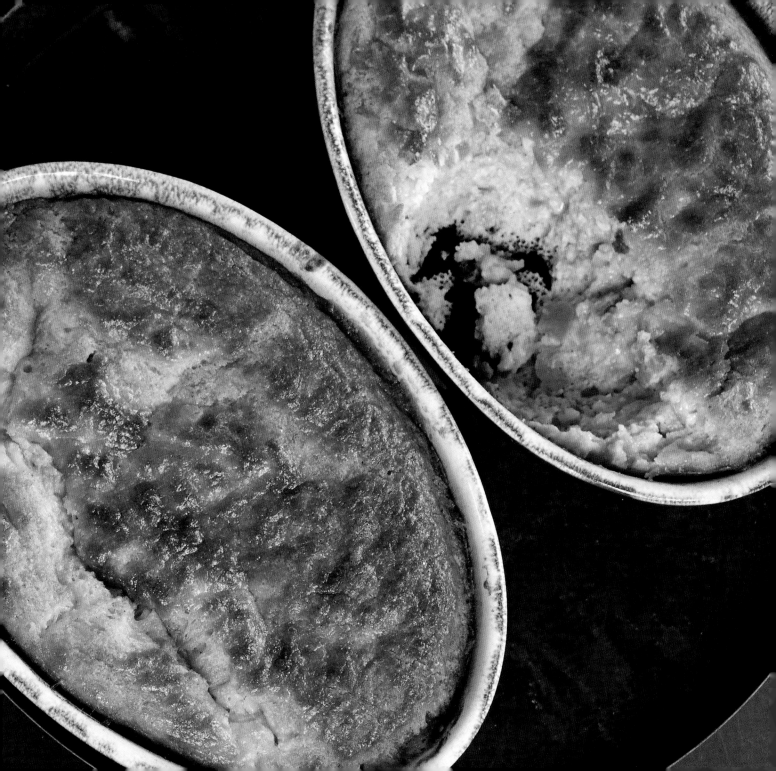

Emily's Souffléed Eggs with Cheddar and Green Chiles

My talented assistant Emily Bell tasted a version of these souffléed eggs at a bed-and-breakfast in Virginia, and she was so impressed by their heavenly light texture that she asked for the recipe. In her kitchen she made a few changes, seasoning the egg and cheese mixture generously with cumin, and creating a colorful tomato and avocado salsa as a garnish.

Serves 8; makes 2 cups/450 g salsa

PREP TIME:
35 minutes

START-TO-FINISH TIME:
1 hour, 30 minutes

MAKE AHEAD:
Yes, partially (the salsa can be prepared ahead)

Tomato-Avocado Salsa

1 cup/245 g diced tomatoes (½-in/12-mm dice)

1 ripe avocado, cut into ½-in/12-mm dice

½ cup/65 g chopped onion

2 tbsp chopped fresh cilantro

¼ tsp grated lime zest

1½ tbsp fresh lime juice

Kosher salt

Freshly ground black pepper

10 large eggs

½ cup/60 g all-purpose flour

1 tsp baking powder

1½ tsp ground cumin

1 tsp kosher salt

Generous 2 cups/200 g grated sharp cheddar cheese

One 24-oz/680-g container small-curd whole-milk cottage cheese

4 tbsp/55 g unsalted butter, melted

One 4½-oz/130-g can diced green chiles, drained well (see Market Note)

🛒 **MARKET NOTE:**
Diced green chiles, which are quite mild, can be found in the international section of most supermarkets, often near the salsas.

1. For the Tomato-Avocado Salsa: Combine the tomatoes, avocado, onion, cilantro, lime zest, lime juice, ½ tsp salt, and ¼ tsp pepper in a medium nonreactive serving bowl; toss well to combine. Taste and season with more salt and pepper if needed. (The salsa can be prepared 2 hours ahead; cover and refrigerate. Bring to room temperature 30 minutes before serving.)

2. Arrange a rack in the middle of the oven and preheat to 350°F/180°C. Generously butter a 9-by-13-in/23-by-33-cm or another shallow 3-qt/2.8-L baking dish.

3. Put the eggs in a food processor or blender and pulse several times until frothy, about 30 seconds. Add the flour, baking powder, cumin, and salt and pulse until combined. Pour the egg mixture into a large bowl. Add the cheddar cheese, cottage cheese, melted butter, and chiles and mix until well combined.

4. Pour the mixture into the prepared baking dish and bake until the eggs are set and golden on top, about 45 minutes. Remove from the oven and cool for 5 minutes. Pass a bowl of the salsa on the side to serve.

Frittata with Caramelized Onions, Tomatoes, and Fresh Herbs

Frittatas are traditionally cooked over low heat in a frying pan on the stove top, and then finished under the broiler. This one—prepared with golden caramelized onions, diced tomatoes, chives, and rosemary—is started on the stove and then baked in the oven.

Serves 4 to 6

PREP TIME:
30 minutes

START-TO-FINISH TIME:
1 hour, 15 minutes

MAKE AHEAD:
No

1½ tbsp unsalted butter

1½ tbsp olive oil

2 medium onions, halved and thinly sliced

8 large eggs

¾ cup/90 g grated Parmesan cheese, preferably Parmigiano-Reggiano

1 cup/175 g seeded and diced tomatoes

1 tbsp chopped fresh rosemary, plus 1 tsp

1 tbsp chopped fresh chives, plus 1 tsp

½ tsp kosher salt

¼ tsp freshly ground black pepper

1 cup/25 g baby arugula, coarsely chopped

½ cup/85 g fresh goat cheese, crumbled or broken into small pieces

1. Arrange a rack in the middle of the oven and preheat to 350°F/180°C.

2. Heat 1 tbsp of the butter and 1 tbsp of the olive oil in a 9- to 10-in/23- to 25-cm ovenproof nonstick frying pan over medium heat. When hot, add the onions and cook, stirring, until they are golden brown, about 15 minutes. Remove the onions to a plate to cool slightly. Set the pan aside.

3. Break the eggs into a large mixing bowl and whisk to blend. Mix in ½ cup/60 g of the Parmesan, the caramelized onions, the tomatoes, the 1 tbsp rosemary, the 1 tbsp chives, salt, and pepper. Whisk well to combine, and then stir in the arugula.

4. In the same frying pan in which the onions were sautéed, heat the remaining ½ tbsp butter and ½ tbsp oil over medium-high heat until hot. Pour in the egg mixture, stir to distribute evenly, and sprinkle the goat cheese over the top. Cook for 1 minute, and carefully transfer the frying pan to the oven. Bake, uncovered, until the eggs are almost set, but still moist in the center, 8 to 10 minutes.

5. Remove the frying pan from the oven and sprinkle the remaining ¼ cup/30 g Parmesan cheese over the frittata. Arrange a rack 4 to 5 in/10 to 12 cm from the broiler, and broil the frittata, with the oven door ajar, watching constantly, until the eggs are set and the cheese has melted, 1 to 2 minutes.

6. Sprinkle the remaining rosemary and chives over the frittata. Cut into wedges and serve hot or at room temperature.

Mushroom Popover Casserole

This dish makes a showstopper entrée for brunch, yet is quite easy to assemble. The rich popover batter is poured into a casserole dish, rather than into popover pans, and rises dramatically up the sides of the dish while in the oven. Then, during the last few minutes of baking, a creamy sauté of mushrooms is added as a filling. Serve this unique popover with a hearty salad (sliced Belgian endive, red leaf lettuce, and walnuts, dressed in a mustard vinaigrette, work particularly well), along with a warm, crusty baguette.

Serves 6 to 8

PREP TIME:
15 minutes

START-TO-FINISH TIME:
1 hour, 25 minutes

MAKE AHEAD:
Yes, partially

Mushroom Filling

4½ tbsp/70 ml olive oil

1 lb/455 g brown mushrooms (cremini), thinly sliced through the stems

1⅓ cups/160 g chopped green onions (including 2 in/5 cm of the green stems)

2 tbsp finely chopped garlic

2 tsp crushed dried rosemary (see Market Note, page 34)

2 tsp dried thyme

Kosher salt

Freshly ground black pepper

½ cup/120 ml mascarpone cheese

Popover

4 tbsp/55 g unsalted butter

1½ cups/175 g all-purpose flour

1 tsp kosher salt

1½ cups/360 ml whole milk

4 large eggs

Grated Parmesan cheese, preferably Parmigiano-Reggiano, for sprinkling

1. Arrange a rack in the middle of the oven and preheat to 450°F/230°C. Have ready a 9-by-13-in/23-by-33-cm baking dish.

2. For the Mushroom Filling: Heat the olive oil in a large, heavy frying pan over medium-high heat until very hot but not smoking. Add the mushrooms and cook, stirring often, until any liquid exuded from the mushrooms has evaporated, 5 to 6 minutes. Add the green onions and garlic and cook, stirring, until the green onions have softened, about 2 minutes. Stir in the rosemary, thyme, ½ tsp salt, and several grinds of pepper. Remove the frying pan from the heat and add the mascarpone, stirring until it has melted. Season the mushrooms with more salt and pepper if needed. (The filling can be prepared 1 day ahead; cool, cover, and refrigerate. Reheat over low heat, stirring.)

3. For the Popover: Put the butter in the baking dish, and put the dish in the oven until the butter has melted and is hot, 5 minutes.

4. Meanwhile, in a medium bowl, mix together the flour and salt. In a large bowl, whisk together the milk and eggs. Add the flour to the egg mixture, whisking until no lumps remain and the batter is smooth.

continued . . .

5. Remove the hot baking dish from the oven and, using potholders, tilt the dish several times to spread the butter evenly over the bottom. Pour the popover batter into the dish; bake 15 minutes. The batter will start to puff up around the edges. Reduce the temperature to 350°F/180°C, and bake for 15 minutes more. At this point, the sides will have puffed up around the edges of the baking dish.

6. Remove the dish from the oven (close the oven door to maintain the temperature). Quickly spoon the mushroom filling over the bottom of the popover. Return to the oven and bake until the mushrooms are very hot, 10 to 12 minutes more.

7. Remove the popover from the oven. With a sharp knife, cut into six to eight portions. Serve hot and pass a bowl of Parmesan cheese for sprinkling.

Roasted Vegetable Flans with Fresh Tarragon

When spring's first bunches of asparagus arrive in the markets, use them to make these delectable breakfast flans. They are prepared with a roasted mélange of vegetables, including the green spears, shiitake mushrooms, and leeks, all bathed in a savory, tarragon-scented custard. Add some warm, crusty rolls and a peppery watercress salad tossed in a vinaigrette dressing to complete the menu.

Serves 4

PREP TIME:
20 minutes

START-TO-FINISH TIME:
1 hour, 15 minutes

MAKE AHEAD:
Yes, partially

8 oz/225 g thin asparagus, tough bases removed, and cut into 1-in/2.5-cm pieces

1 medium leek (white and light green parts only), halved lengthwise, and cut into ½-in-/12-mm-thick slices

4 oz/115 g shiitake mushrooms, stemmed and cut into ½-in-/12-mm-wide strips

¼ cup/60 ml olive oil

Kosher salt

Freshly ground black pepper

4 large eggs

1½ cups/360 ml half-and-half

½ cup/120 ml crème fraîche, homemade (see page 12) or store-bought

5 tsp chopped fresh tarragon

1 tsp grated lemon zest

1¼ cups/100 g grated Gruyère cheese

1. Arrange a rack in the middle of the oven and preheat to 400°F/200°C. Butter four 5½-in/14-cm gratin or crème brûlée dishes and place them on a rimmed baking sheet.

2. Spread the asparagus, leek, and mushrooms in a single layer on a large, rimmed baking sheet. Drizzle with the olive oil and toss to coat well. Season the vegetables with salt and several grinds of pepper.

3. Roast the vegetables in the oven until tender and lightly browned around the edges, about 20 minutes, stirring after the first 10 minutes with a wooden spoon. Remove from the oven and divide the vegetables evenly among the four prepared gratins. (The vegetables can be roasted 1 hour ahead; cover the dishes loosely with foil and leave at cool room temperature.)

4. In a large mixing bowl, whisk the eggs until blended. Add the half-and-half, crème fraîche, 1 tsp of the chopped tarragon, the lemon zest, ½ tsp kosher salt, and several grinds of pepper. Whisk well to combine, and stir in 1 cup/80 g of the Gruyère. Divide the mixture evenly among the four gratins. Sprinkle each flan with 1 tbsp of the remaining cheese. Bake until set, about 30 minutes.

5. Sprinkle each flan with 1 tsp of the remaining tarragon. Serve warm.

Potato and Chorizo Tortilla

This Spanish-inspired tortilla is a snap to assemble and makes a tempting main course for breakfast or brunch. The casserole is composed of sliced Yukon golds, sautéed onions and chorizo, and grated Manchego, all topped with a savory egg custard. A green salad of baby spinach or arugula with grape tomatoes, tossed in a sherry or red wine vinaigrette, and a crusty loaf of country bread would be easy accompaniments.

Serves 4

PREP TIME:
25 minutes

START-TO-FINISH TIME:
1 hour, 30 minutes

MAKE AHEAD:
Yes

Kosher salt

1½ lb/680 g Yukon gold potatoes, peeled and cut into ¼-in-/6-mm-thick slices

3 tbsp olive oil

2 cups/250 g chopped onion

6 oz/170 g Spanish-style chorizo, halved lengthwise and thinly sliced (⅛ in/3 mm or less; see Market Note, page 99)

6 large eggs

⅓ cup/75 ml sour cream

Freshly ground black pepper

1 cup/70 g shredded Manchego cheese

1 tbsp finely chopped fresh flat-leaf parsley

1. Arrange a rack in the middle of the oven and preheat to 350°F/180°C. Generously oil a 2-qt/2-L baking dish.

2. Bring a large pot of water to boil, and add 2 tsp salt and the potato slices. Cook for 5 minutes, or until barely tender when pierced with a knife. Drain well.

3. Heat the olive oil in a medium, heavy frying pan over medium heat. When hot, add the onion and chorizo and cook, stirring frequently, until the onion is softened and the chorizo has taken on some color, 5 to 6 minutes. Remove from the heat.

4. In a medium bowl, whisk together the eggs, sour cream, and ½ tsp salt.

5. Put half of the potatoes in the prepared dish and season generously with salt and pepper. Spread the onion and chorizo mixture evenly over the potatoes, and sprinkle with half of the Manchego cheese. Top with the remaining potatoes, seasoning them generously with salt and pepper. Pour the egg mixture over the ingredients in the dish, making sure the potatoes are covered. Sprinkle the remaining cheese on top.

6. Bake, uncovered, until the potatoes are very tender when pierced with a knife, the eggs are set, and the top is golden, 40 to 45 minutes. (The tortilla can be baked 4 hours ahead; cool, cover, and refrigerate. Reheat, uncovered, in a preheated 350°F/180°C oven until hot, 15 to 20 minutes.) Sprinkle the tortilla with the parsley and serve warm or at room temperature.

Gratin of Eggs, Italian Sausage, and Sun-Dried Tomatoes

Over the years, I've included this golden egg gratin in more than a few brunch classes, and students have always responded to it enthusiastically. They are delighted that it is so quick, easy, and inexpensive. But best of all, they like the harmonious blend of Italian flavors and the extra-creamy texture of this dish.

Serves 6

PREP TIME:
15 minutes

START-TO-FINISH TIME:
1 hour, 10 minutes

MAKE AHEAD:
No

1 lb/455 g sweet Italian sausage
  (see Cooking Tip)

½ cup/50 g chopped shallots

2 tsp finely chopped garlic

½ cup/70 g chopped sun-dried tomatoes
  packed in oil, drained

4 tbsp/8 g chopped fresh flat-leaf parsley

Kosher salt

5 large eggs, plus 3 egg yolks

2 cups/480 ml half-and-half

2 cups/180 g grated Italian fontina cheese

COOKING TIP:

This casserole is best when prepared with traditional sweet Italian sausage made with pork, but you can use a lower-fat Italian sausage made with chicken. If using the latter, you will need to use 2 to 3 tbsp olive oil for sautéing the sausage.

1. Arrange a rack in the middle of the oven and preheat to 375°F/190°C. Generously butter a 9-by-13-in/23-by-33-cm or another shallow 3-qt/2.8-L baking dish.

2. Remove the casing from the sausage, break the sausages into small pieces, and put in a heavy, medium frying pan over medium heat. Sauté the sausage until it has browned well, stirring and breaking it into very small pieces with a wooden spoon, 4 to 5 minutes. Remove the frying pan from the heat and carefully spoon off all but 1 tbsp of the drippings that have collected in the pan.

3. Return the frying pan with the sausage to medium heat, add the shallots and garlic, and cook, stirring, for 3 minutes. Add the sun-dried tomatoes and 2 tbsp of the parsley, and cook, stirring, for 1 minute more. Taste the sausage mixture and season with salt if needed. Spread on the bottom of the prepared baking dish.

4. Whisk the eggs, egg yolks, half-and-half, and three-quarters of the Fontina together and pour over the sausage. Mix with a spoon, and sprinkle the remaining Fontina on top.

5. Bake, uncovered, until the gratin is golden brown and a knife inserted in the center comes out clean, 25 to 30 minutes. Remove from the oven and cool for 5 minutes. Sprinkle the gratin with the remaining 2 tbsp parsley and serve.

Croissant, Ham, and Mustard Gratin

One of my guilty pleasures is croissants, which I buy with abandon at the local farmers' market in my small New England town and at neighborhood *boulangeries* during stays in Paris. Since I tend to purchase far too many, there are always leftovers, which, I've discovered, can be used in this breakfast casserole. Bite-size pieces of these buttery rolls, diced ham, and some grated cheese are combined with a savory custard, and then baked until the custard is set and the top is golden.

Serves 6

PREP TIME:
10 minutes

START-TO-FINISH TIME:
1 hour

MAKE AHEAD
No

5 croissants, preferably day-old

1 cup/210 g good-quality baked ham, cut into ¼-in/6-mm dice

1 cup/80 g grated Gruyère cheese

2 cups/480 ml whole milk

⅔ cup/165 ml crème fraîche, homemade (see page 12) or store-bought

2 large eggs, plus 2 egg yolks

2 tbsp Dijon mustard

½ tsp kosher salt

Freshly ground black pepper

⅛ tsp freshly grated nutmeg

1. Arrange a rack in the middle of the oven and preheat to 350°F/180°C. Generously butter a 9-by-13-in/23-by-33-cm or another shallow 3-qt/2.8-L baking dish.

2. Cut the croissants into 1-in/2.5-cm pieces to yield 6 cups/ 210 g (you may have some left over). Place on a large rimmed baking sheet and bake until the pieces are dried out and lightly browned, 8 to 10 minutes, depending on the freshness of the croissants. Remove from the oven and spread the pieces in a single layer in the prepared baking dish. Sprinkle the ham and half of the Gruyère over the croissants.

3. In a large bowl, whisk together the milk, crème fraîche, eggs, egg yolks, mustard, salt, several grinds of pepper, and the nutmeg. Ladle the mixture over the croissants, and sprinkle with the remaining cheese.

4. Bake, uncovered, until the custard is set, 35 to 40 minutes. Remove from the oven and cool for 5 minutes before serving.

Baked French Toast with Apples, Apricots, and Cherries

One of the challenges for many cooks is figuring out what to serve overnight company for breakfast or brunch. A dish that is simple to prepare, can be assembled in advance, and delivers a bit of dazzle is the perfect solution. This recipe for baked French toast, topped with a glorious mix of fresh and dried fruits, is that kind of morning entrée. Crispy bacon or sliced ham, fresh juice, plus pots of coffee and tea would make fine accompaniments.

Serves 6

PREP TIME:
1 hour, 20 minutes or more, including time to soak the bread

START-TO-FINISH TIME:
2 hours, 20 minutes or more

MAKE AHEAD:
Yes, partially

1 one- to two-day-old loaf good-quality artisan-style country bread

2½ cups/600 ml store-bought eggnog (see Cooking Tip)

Apple, Apricot, and Cherry Topping

8 tbsp/115 g unsalted butter

½ cup/100 g light brown sugar

1 tsp ground cinnamon

1¾ lb/800 g Granny Smith apples, peeled, cored, and cut into ½-in-/12-mm-thick wedges

¾ cup/140 g dried apricots, cut into ½-in/12-mm dice

¼ cup/40 g dried sour cherries

¾ tsp grated lemon zest

½ cup/55 g coarsely chopped walnuts

1 tbsp unsalted butter, melted

COOKING TIP:

I often serve this dish during the Christmas holidays, when eggnog is available in all the supermarkets; it's a big time-saver. If you can't find any, whisk together 4 egg yolks, ½ cup/100 g sugar, and 2 cups/480 ml light cream to blend. Measure 2½ cups/600 ml for the recipe.

1. Generously butter a 9-by-13-in/23-by-33-cm or another shallow 3-qt/2.8-L baking dish.

2. Cut the ends off the bread, and cut the loaf into ¾-in-/2-cm-thick slices. Cut large slices in half and arrange the bread on the bottom of the baking dish in a single tight layer. (Save the ends and any extra slices for another use.) Pour the eggnog evenly over the bread. Cover the dish with plastic wrap and refrigerate for at least 1 hour, preferably overnight.

3. For the Apple, Apricot, and Cherry Topping: Melt the butter in a large, heavy frying pan over medium heat. When hot, add the brown sugar and cinnamon and cook, stirring, for 1 minute to combine. Add the apple wedges and cook, stirring often, until slightly softened, 4 to 5 minutes. Add the apricots, cherries, and lemon zest and cook for 1 minute more. (The apple mixture can be prepared 1 day ahead; cool, cover, and refrigerate. Reheat before using.)

4. When ready to bake, arrange a rack in the middle of the oven and preheat to 375°F/190°C.

5. Remove the baking dish with the bread slices from the refrigerator and turn the slices over. Spoon the fruit mixture evenly over them, and sprinkle with the walnuts. Bake until the apples are tender when pierced with a sharp knife and lightly browned around the edges, about 40 minutes. Cool for 5 minutes. Brush the top of the casserole with the melted butter. Serve warm.

THE CASEROLE DIRECTORY

PERFECT FOR A CROWD

Lelia's Venetian Chicken with Porcini Mushrooms and Fontina (page 28)

Baked Chicken, Fennel, and Tomatoes (page 20)

Cornmeal-Coated Chicken with Ancho Chiles, Beans, and Corn (page 23)

Provençal Daube de Boeuf with Olives, Tomatoes, and Orange (page 42)

Cassoulet Rapide (page 53)

New Orleans Shrimp and Andouille Jambalaya (page 66)

Only Vegetables Moussaka (page 86)

Corn, Leek, and Chorizo Pudding (page 99)

Wild Mushroom Lasagna (page 145)

Rigatoni with Spicy Tomato Sauce, Kalamatas, and Two Cheeses (page 139)

MOVEABLE FEASTS

GREAT FOR TRAVELING, POTLUCKS, AND TAILGATES

Cornmeal-Coated Chicken with Ancho Chiles, Beans, and Corn (page 23)

Chicken, Sweet Potato, and Bacon Casserole (page 18)

Turkey and Corn Tortilla Casserole with Lime-Scented Sour Cream (page 32)

Cold Nights Sausage and Potato Gratin (page 50)

Pasta Spirals with Ricotta and Prosciutto (page 142)

Rigatoni with Spicy Tomato Sauce, Kalamatas, and Two Cheeses (page 139)

CASSEROLES FOR HOLIDAYS

CHRISTMAS

Wild Mushroom Lasagna (page 145) for Christmas Eve

Baked French Toast with Apples, Apricots, and Cherries (page 169) for Christmas morning

THANKSGIVING

Turkey with Red and Green Grapes on Walnut Polenta (page 33)

After Thanksgiving, Turkey Shepherd's Pie (page 114)

Creamed Turkey, Fall Vegetables, and Wild Rice Bake (page 30) for after Thanksgiving

MARDI GRAS

New Orleans Shrimp and Andouille Jambalaya (page 66)

ST. PATRICK'S DAY

Corned Beef and Cabbage with Country Mustard Sauce (page 44)

EASTER

Salmon Baked with Spring Vegetables and Fresh Herbs (page 78)

Lamb and Spinach Phyllo Pie (page 122)

JULY FOURTH

New England Lobster and Corn Casserole (page 73)

Corn, Leek, and Chorizo Pudding (page 99)

CASSEROLES TO MAKE AND BAKE IN ABOUT ONE HOUR

Turkey with Red and Green Grapes on Walnut Polenta (page 33)

Turkey Cutlets Baked with Gruyère and Onions (page 36)

Saffron Rice Pilaf with Lamb Meatballs, Red Peppers, and Dates (page 58)

Cod and Red-Skin Potato Gratins (page 80)

Baked Fish on a Bed of Spinach, Chickpeas, and Tomatoes (page 76)

Creamed Peas and Spring Onions with Buttered Bread Crumbs (page 88)

Swiss Chard, Mascarpone, and Cherry Tomato Gratin (page 90)

Individual Broccoli and Cauliflower Cheddar Gratins (page 92)

Shrimp, Tomatoes, and Artichokes Under Saffron Croutons (page 128)

Emily's Souffléed Eggs with Cheddar and Green Chiles (page 158)

Gratin of Eggs, Italian Sausage, and Sun-Dried Tomatoes (page 166)

Croissant, Ham, and Mustard Gratin (page 167)

CASSEROLES FOR DAYS WHEN YOU HAVE EXTRA TIME TO SPEND IN THE KITCHEN

EASY ON THE POCKET

WORTH A SPLURGE

HEALTHFUL EATING

CASSEROLES THAT FREEZE WELL

INDEX